GARDEN OPEN TOMORROW

Open garden day at Sudbrook Cottage; Beverley Nichols looks on while his factotum, Reginald Gaskin, takes money for charity. Courtesy of the Bryan Connon Collection.

GARDEN OPEN TOMORROW

Beverley Nichols

Prologue by Bryan Connon

TIMBER PRESS
Portland, Oregon

TIMBER PRESS, INC.
The Haseltine Building
133 S.W. Second Avenue, Suite 450
Portland, Oregon 97204, U.S.A.

ISBN 0-88192-552-7

Printed in Hong Kong

Reprinted 2003

A catalog record for this book is available from
the Library of Congress

CONTENTS

DISCLAIMER

THIS BOOK was originally published in 1968 and mentions many merchants, products, and prices of the time. Few of the nurseries mentioned in the book persist today, and most of the products and trade names are of period interest only. Please note that chemical formulations and applications recommended by Mr. Nichols are of dubious validity today. Some are even prohibited by current regulation. Some names of plants have changed in the previous forty years; updated names and synonyms are provided in the index for the reader's convenience. Notwithstanding the above, Mr. Nichols's various enthusiasms and colorful descriptions of plants and gardening practices may be safely regarded as being timeless.

PROLOGUE

Sudbrook Cottage, the setting for Garden Open Tomorrow, *was Nichols's home and garden from* 1958 *until his death in* 1983. *Nichols had reluctantly departed in late* 1957 *or early* 1958 *from Merry Hall, the spacious residence that figures in the trilogy of books with the same name. As an attempt to economize, he moved to a four-room flat in Fitzjohns Avenue, Hampstead, which proved to be a terrible disappointment. Bryan Connon continues the story in* Beverley Nichols: A Life, *which is excepted here with his kind permission.*

After a few months in Fitzjohns Avenue [in 1958], it was agreed that they [Nichols; his partner, Cyril Butcher; the cats; and his factotum, Reginald Gaskin] must leave. . . .

Quite unexpectedly, fate offered the solution. A wealthy lady friend of Beverley's noticed that a pleasant-sounding property in Richmond was up for auction. Somewhat reluctantly, he agreed to go to see it, fully expecting to be disappointed. He was, on the contrary, delighted and amazed. In the late eighteenth century the Duke of Argyll had built a block of six cottages to accommodate workers on his estate, Sudbrook Park. At the western end, the sixth cottage was tucked away at the back of the block which then continued with stables to form a right-angled spur. This and the cottage on the corner had been knocked into one dwelling and christened Sudbrook Cottage. The Duke had not stinted on space and when a central staircase had been taken out and the rooms on either side of it combined, the result was a surprisingly large drawing-room. There were a further four rooms on the ground floor, together with a cloakroom, kitchen and a store-room fashioned from the stables, all in perfect condition. Upstairs were two bathrooms and four bedrooms.

Even better was the walled garden which was astonishingly large for a cottage, just under an acre, the size indicating that it might originally have been the vegetable garden for the 'Big House', or perhaps a paddock for horses. When Beverley first saw it, it was an uncompromising rectangle given over to grass with flower borders and dominated by a massive topiary bird hacked out of box. A similar creature, though not as large, dominated the small garden facing the road. These, Beverley decided, must go to leave a blank canvas on which a new garden could be designed. His mind raced ahead with possibilities—but how was he to acquire the property?

His wealthy friend came to the rescue. It was a Crown property with a lease of nearly forty years to run; she would buy the lease, and make it over to Beverley who would then repay her over a set period with minimal interest. Her only condition was that her action should not be made known publicly. At auction, bidding began at £3,000 and rapidly rose to £7,850. For a time, it was touch and go whether she would acquire it, but she had given her representative a free hand, and although Beverley's heart sank as the price went up, in the end he became, by her generosity, the owner.

In the summer of 1958, he left the hated Fitzjohns Avenue flat and moved into Sudbrook Cottage, which remained his home until his death. . . . Economy was forgotten as he began planning the new garden, helped by Kenneth Page whom Beverley considered to be the most knowledgeable gardener he had ever employed. Beverley provided the overall design and Mr Page interpreted it, supplying many suggestions of his own. After clearing the ground and ceremoniously burning the topiary monsters, the first step was to divide the garden in half, thus giving the impression that it was twice its real size. The second step was to make water an important feature, as at Merry Hall, but more informally, to suit Sudbrook Cottage. In the further section of the halved space a pond was dug and the earth dispersed to raise sections of the garden. Then, following another Nichols precept, they dug new curved beds so that the original straight lines of the rectangle were obscured. To mark the boundary between the two sections, two magnificent porphyry urns were placed on brick pillars. Several old fruit trees were left intact during the clearance, as well as a superb copper beech to one side of the ground. The new planting concentrated on colourful shrubs including rhododendrons; bedding plants were kept to a minimum and instead there was a liberal use of perennials. . . .

In 1963 came the first book about the garden at Sudbrook Cottage. Unlike the Thatch Cottage and Merry Hall books, it was primarily concerned with the practicalities of gardening and in this respect may have disappointed those readers who expected the usual dominating parade of amusing characters and anecdotes. These were present, but very much in the background. It seemed that Beverley now wished to establish himself as a practical gardener and to kill off any impression that he was merely a theorist 'playing at it'. He had previously disguised the fact that he had avoided all the back-breaking chores but in his sixties he could concede that others did the hard work while he confined himself (as he always had done) to the lighter tasks. But in more than thirty years of gardening he had acquired a sound knowledge, and even experts might learn a thing or two from this book. Implicit in the title that Beverley chose, *Garden Open Today*, was a challenge to his peers to come and see for themselves what he had achieved in only a few years. . . .

In the following year *Forty Favourite Flowers* was published. While not claiming to be an addendum to *Garden Open Today*, for practical purposes that is what it was. As usual, the text was entertaining and was packed with advice, but the illustrations were in black and white rather than in colour, which disappointed Beverley and, he believed, lost potential sales. . . .

[Several years later], he completed work on a sequel to *Garden Open Today* called *Garden Open Tomorrow*. It was greeted with pleasure by garden-lovers when it appeared in December 1968 and it solved the problem of Christmas buying for many. Four years after this, it was republished in a special edition for the Country Book Club. It was very much the mixture as before —sound advice blended with familiar touches of satire, wit and sentiment, the pages again decorated with drawings by William McLaren. Fred Whitsey, the authority on gardening, reviewed the book for the *Sunday Telegraph*. 'I read it straight through because I couldn't stop', he wrote, and ended, 'I added to my store of knowledge by way of the reportage of the author's own gardening experiences, and again and again I found myself nodding with that satisfying sense one gets from whole-hearted agreement'.

GARDEN OPEN TOMORROW

Facsimile of the Original Edition of 1968

GARDEN OPEN TOMORROW

Beverley Nichols

With Drawings by William McLaren

Heinemann : London

To the Memory
   of
Certain Feline Companions
   who
While this Work was being Completed
   were
Constantly by the Author's Side
Not only in the Garden
   but
At his Desk
Giving to his Words
The Approval of their muted Purrs
   and
The Authority of their muddy Paws

CONTENTS

ACKNOWLEDGEMENTS

MY thanks are due to the following gardeners who have assisted me, directly or indirectly, in the compilation of this book, by granting special facilities to explore their own gardens, public or private, and in some cases accompanying me on these explorations:

Lord Aberconway, President of the Royal Horticultural Society, and his head gardener at Bodnant, Mr Charles Puddle.

Sir Eric Savill, Director of Forestry and Gardens for the Crown Estate of Windsor.

The late Sir Frederick Stern, Vice-President of the Royal Horticultural Society, author of *A Chalk Garden* and other authoritative works.

Mr F. P. Knight, Director of the R.H.S. Gardens at Wisley.

Messrs Lanning Roper and Fred Whitsey, the correspondents of the *Sunday Times* and the *Sunday Telegraph*.

Also to many professional nurserymen with whom I have corresponded since the publication of *Garden Open Today*.

In every case where direct mention is made in the text of the gardens which these gentlemen own or control, they have been kind enough to check the manuscript, but they are in no way responsible for the opinions expressed therein.

CHAPTER ONE

WINTER'S RAGES

'THE WEATHER IN ENGLAND'—so wrote my friends with monotonous persistence throughout the cruel winter—'is quite indescribable.' Whereupon they proceeded in great detail to describe it.

I was out of it all, lecturing in America, where the weather, so they assumed, was not 'indescribable'. In a sense, they were right. It would have been easy, for example, to write a graphic description of the tornado which hit Detroit at fourteen below zero, at the precise moment of my arrival, lifting me bodily into the air and depositing me in a gutter full of slush, whence I was removed to hospital in an ambulance, X-rayed, bandaged, and inoculated against lockjaw.

This last precaution, presumably, was taken in order that my teeth might not suddenly clamp together, with a loud snap, on the lecture platform where I was due an hour later.

Equally easy would it have been to describe the cruel cold that was gripping the Middle West. 'How deep does the frost go down?' I asked a lady from Cleveland after one of the lectures. She had been sitting in the front row, dressed in deep black, and she had been slightly distracting, because she looked as if she had lost something. Her answer showed that this was indeed the case. 'I know it goes down at least four feet,' she replied, 'because I've just been burying my cook.' But those monarchs of the American stage, Alfred Lunt and Lynn Fontanne, could do even better. The frost, in their garden, they declared, went down much deeper than that, and they did not have to resort to such extreme measures as burying the cook in order to prove it.

Such details I kept to myself, in letters home, for as the weeks went by it was evident that things were indeed pretty bad. In isolated districts the troops were being called out; on Dartmoor the ponies were dying in their tracks; and at Richmond, only a few miles from my cottage, the Thames was frozen solid for the first time in recorded history. So, as it happened, was the Mississippi; but in America one expects these things, in England one does not. In England the climate is often cheerless and always unpredictable, but seldom melodramatic. One of the details that evoked most vividly the plight of my friends at home came in a letter from an old lady who lived in a lonely cottage on the Sussex downs. She had been distressed by the plight of the birds. She had been feeding them as far as possible, though it had been difficult, because sometimes the country lanes were impassable for days on end. And yet the birds had been growing weaker and weaker; some of them, after pecking their crusts and their bacon rinds, had scarcely the strength to fly away.

'But now,' she wrote, 'I realize how foolish I have been. It was not only food they needed, but water. So I have fixed up a contrivance of buckets, with little night-lights hanging over them, which give just enough heat to keep the water from freezing. It is a *great* success, and I only pray that the supply of night-lights will hold out.' This was the last letter I ever had from her. A few days later she was found outside the door of her cottage, where she had slipped and fallen. By her side was a packet of night-lights, encased in solid ice. As long as there are such characters in the old country I think that England, in spite of its climate, is not such a bad place in which to live.

But what of the garden?

This was the question one asked with increasing urgency, as the letters continued to pour in, with stories tragic, stories comic, and stories almost unbelievable. As a gardener I had a very personal reason for asking it, because ever since I first walked down the garden path I have had an almost obsessional interest in winter flowers. It had been my proud boast that in every garden I had ever made, on every single day of the year, I had been able to pick a bunch of outdoor flowers for my desk, even if only a cluster of *Iris unguicularis* (syn. *I. stylosa*) picked in bud from under a snow drift. (In spite of years of propaganda on my part there are still all too many gardeners who neglect to plant these flowers which, quite literally, can be rescued from drifts two feet deep and brought indoors to open their orchidaceous petals within the hour.) But what if the drifts were *five* feet deep, as apparently they were in some places, and what if the frost had clawed its way below the roots? My friend and factotum of many years' standing, Mr Gaskin, had written to tell me that he had been obliged to dig his way across the lawn to the greenhouse, as though to a beleaguered fortress. He had added as a matter of even more urgent importance that how he was going to continue coping with the sanitary problems of Four and Five he did *not* know.

Four and Five are my feline companions, aged sixteen and eighteen respectively.[1] Normally, during a cold spell, when the earth is frozen, they make use of the piles of anthracite in the tool-shed, from which they emerge with black paws and faintly haughty expressions, like ladies in restaurants where the powder-rooms are not of the highest standard. But now the anthracite was an iron, icy mass, so they had been obliged to use the sand-box, which they were accustomed to spurn. But even that had frozen, with the result that Four had 'done something' in the bath-tub. This was indeed front-page news, and the story was made all the more dramatic by the fact that the bath in which Four had 'done something' had an icicle a foot long protruding from the hot tap.

After such extremities, would there be anything left of the garden at all even though the thaw had begun at last? Well . . . one would soon know.

The flight to England was uneventful, or rather it seemed uneventful, thanks to the soothing influence of a magic potion prescribed by my friend Dr Morgenbesser, of New

---

[1] If the reader has glanced at the Dedication he will realize that Four and Five are no longer with us. They were of a great age when they departed from this world; Four was nineteen and Five sighed himself to sleep on his twenty-first birthday. But they both linger so vividly in my memory that I do not care to write of them in the past tense.

York City. This remarkable elixir looks and tastes like *crème de menthe*, but its effect is far more beneficent; after a single sip of it, even though the plane is obviously about to explode, one relaxes in one's seat with a smile which, to the undrugged observer, must appear faintly owlish. 'There is no cause for alarm,' crackles the voice of the pilot over the loudspeakers —a remark which is normally calculated to strike terror into the staunchest heart. But now, one nods in a haze of amiable agreement. How *could* there be any cause for alarm? One of the engines has failed, lightning is streaking round the fuselage, there is a strong smell of petrol, and emerging from the rear are some very peculiar noises, which cannot be solely attributed to the party of drunken Russians who boarded the plane at the last moment, probably equipped with infernal machines. But *alarm*? What a curious notion! Nothing is alarming; God's in His heaven; and death, where is thy sting? One's chin sinks forward, and just before falling asleep one wonders why one is apparently wearing three safety belts, each of them slightly blurred.

But I was supposed to be writing a gardening book. So let us land at London Airport, towards midnight, by the light of a brilliant moon, let us motor through the narrow winding streets, experiencing all the sensations familiar to the returning wanderer, let us turn down the tree-lined avenue on the deserted common and open the lattice gate that leads into the tiny courtyard outside the front door. And then, before we reach for our latch-key or switch on the light, let us bend down, grope with cold fingers in the sodden earth, catch hold of the stump of a much-loved plant, and give a long, long tug.

And then—let us breathe a sigh of relief. For when we tugged, the stump resisted fiercely. It was firm as a rock.

Things, maybe, were not quite so bad as we expected.

This curious conduct, I suspect, is typical of the returning traveller when the traveller is a gardener. The urge to see what has been happening in the flower-beds sweeps aside all other considerations. I once knew a man whose wife threatened him with divorce because of this very thing. He had been away for three months and in his absence she had presented him with a baby. She perversely supposed that his first action, on returning home, would be to come to her room in order to pay his respects to her, and it. Not at all. He found it of more immediate importance to hurry across the lawn to inspect a recently planted *Embothrium coccineum*. This behaviour she found unnatural; some women have no sense of priorities.

Now for our stump, which refused to budge. The reason why it was so important was because it was a branch of lemon verbena (*Lippia citriodora*), and this plant has the reputation of being hardy only in the most sheltered areas of our island. If it had succumbed after all these months of arctic weather the roots would certainly have been destroyed, and it would have come out of the ground like a rotten tooth, for, as we have seen, the thaw was already well advanced. The fact that it stayed firm was a happy augury for a whole range of other plants whose possible demise was troubling me.

And here, while we are still standing on the doorstep, let us pause to remind gardeners of a lesson they are often inclined to forget:

PRACTICAL NOTE

Every year, in thousands of gardens all over the country, valuable plants are hacked down and dug up and chucked on to the rubbish heap because their owners are under the mistaken impression that they are dead when, in fact, they are very much alive. This tragedy could be averted if gardeners, instead of using the familiar technique of scratching the bark to see if it shows green underneath, would simply bend down and tug, and go on tugging. Consider our lemon verbena. All through the following spring and most of the summer it looked as dead as a doornail; the solitary stump above the ground showed no sign of life whatsoever; and most people would have dug it up and thrown it away. But we went on tugging, and every tug reassured us that somewhere under the ground there was life, and that the plant was fighting to survive. Finally, towards the end of July, we were rewarded by a small green leaf, which seemed to send out an even sweeter fragrance than usual, as though it wished to show its appreciation of our patience.

This experience was repeated, time and again, all over the garden. Perhaps the most striking example was afforded by a group of pernettyas, which looked so moribund that they cast a gloom around them. Tugging revealed that the roots were alive, but since the main branches seemed obviously dead, and showed brown when we scratched the bark, I wanted to cut them off and start again from ground level. Mr Page dissuaded me from doing so, and sure enough, by the end of June, even these brown 'dead' branches were breaking into shrill green leaf.

The moral: Never give up hope until you have proof positive that a plant is dead, even if you have to wait through most of the year. And go on tugging.

We are still pausing in the porch, with the garden waiting for us, dreaming in the moonlight, with maybe a few patches of snow lingering in some sheltered corners. And though we are anxious to know what has been going on in our absence, we might linger a little longer before opening the door, for we seem to have talked ourselves into a practical frame of mind, and one never knows—at least I never do—how long such a mood will persist. So let us make the most of it while it lasts. For our experiment with the lemon verbena has a lesson to teach us of very wide importance, and we might as well learn it here and now.

At the risk of sounding perverse I would suggest that this fierce winter, from the gardener's point of view, did a lot more good than harm, if only because it added so largely to our stock of knowledge. It forced us to revise many accepted notions about the comparative hardiness of a whole host of

plants; indeed, some of these revisions of opinion have been so drastic that many authors of horticultural works, including the nurserymen, will have to do a great deal of re-writing if their statements are to have any contemporary application.

Let me illustrate this from my own garden, beginning with the fuchsias. I have just been doing some homework on these lovely flowers and, with only one exception, all the experts insist that during the winter months—and they were writing, remember, of an average winter—fuchsias should be given the protection of leaves, or ashes, or both. (The exception is a certain nurseryman who is so dewy-eyed about his wares that he would persuade you to try growing cacti on icebergs if he thought he could make a sale. All the others were unanimous about this need for protection, and several dropped ominous hints about their preference for sheltered districts not too far from the sea.)

Well . . . my fuchsias got no protection at all and after the winter they made a sturdier growth than they have ever made before. Admittedly, the majority of them are planted in reasonably congenial surroundings, in the shadow of an old pear tree; but they still get their fair share of the cruel east winds, which drive home the bitter argument of the frost. However, they were not given the solace of a single teacup of ashes, nor a solitary spray of bracken. This was in no way due to any negligence on the part of Mr Page. For weeks on end he was physically marooned in Leatherhead, and by the time he was able to fight his way back to the garden through the blizzards, he concluded, not unnaturally, that the fuchsias had had it. But they hadn't. And here, for the benefit of the fuchsia-lover, are the varieties which stood up, naked and unarmed, to an ordeal which is unlikely to be parallelled within the lifetime of any of us.

Our Fuchsias

Varieties which are generally recognized as hardy in normal winters:
Graf Witte—scarlet and violet-purple.
Madame Cornelissen—crimson and white.
Mrs Popple—scarlet and deep purple.
Alice Hoffman—cerise and white.
Tom Thumb—cerise and mauve.

Varieties which are generally recognized as only semi-hardy:
Fascination—bright red and rose-pink.
Achievement—bright cerise and purple magenta.
Mrs Marshall—creamy-white and rosy-cerise.
Rose of Castile—white and violet-purple.

Variegated foliage:
Fuchsia gracilis variegata.

So much for the 'experts'. Of course, if you have a specially tender heart, you can go on giving fuchsias the recommended covering of ashes. However, in the modern world there are so many melancholy occasions when the scattering of ashes is called for that I should have thought that most people would not wish to indulge in this ceremony unless they were positively compelled to do so.

If the stern discipline of the winter opened our eyes to the fact that many plants are hardier than their reputation, it opened them even more widely to the fact that an equal number are not so tough as we had imagined.

Consider the peerless family of the rhododendrons. The 'common' rhododendron, the genus from which all the long line of aristocrats is derived, is, of course, the species *ponticum* which purples our woods in June. Some horticultural snobs sneer at the ponticum, and some silly women say that the colour is 'vulgar'—an observation which betrays their own coarseness of fibre, for few sights could be lovelier than a drift of ponticums shining through a mist of silver birches; it is as though Manet had taken a picture by Corot and lightened it with the fires of his own more vivid brush.

However, 'common' or not, the ponticums showed none of the toughness that might have been expected from those who came—as it were—of peasant stock; all over the British Isles it was they who suffered most. Some were killed out-right, others were so browned and blasted that throughout the summer they were an affront to the eye. Meanwhile, their blue-blooded relations, in particular the lovely group of *x Loderi*, were shrugging the snow from their branches with elegant disdain.

Here is a case in point. When I opened the garden last May, the shrub that stole the show was a very finely grown specimen of *Rhododendron x Loderi* King George. As we stood looking at it, before the crowds came in, Mr Page remarked, 'If anybody had told me last February that this shrub would be looking like this today I should have suggested that he was talking through his hat. Four months ago the leaves were clenched as tight as a fist, the branches were weighed down with snow, and more snow, which froze solid. . . . I can tell you, it nearly broke my heart. And now . . . look at her!'

There was no need for this injunction; she was all too easy to look at. Once again the branches were laden with snow, but it was the snow of blossom, as white as moonlit silk; and the leaves, which spread with tropical luxuriance, were misted with a grape-like bloom. She was as lovely as any bride and why she was ever named after King George V is one of the mysteries of horticultural nomenclature. For that monarch, though impeccable in his private, and estimable in his public life, was scarcely a figure of romance. He evokes a vision of beards and battleships, and such echoes of his voice as remain to us have little melody. Whereas this ravishing creature seems to make the air sing around her. One day somebody should write a chapter on the naming of flowers, if only to deplore the fact that so many exquisite blossoms carry the names of women who sound as if they had spent their entire lives bending over the kitchen sink.

The practical mood is wearing off. In a moment we will recapture it, but first I would like to indulge in the luxury of explaining one of the many reasons why rhododendrons have, for me, so unique an enchantment. We all know—or ought to know—that as the flowers fade and die they must be nipped off at the base in order to stimulate next year's growth. This nipping, of course, is known as 'dead-heading'. But sometimes I slightly anticipate the process by shaking the branches, so that some of the petals fall to the ground before their time. If one does this, one immediately steps into a realm of magic. The petals drop from the noble flowers, spilling on to the earth in patterns of pink and white and ivory and scarlet; and then one bends down and gently rearranges them, as though one were kneeling at the feet of a beautiful lady, moving the folds of her dress while she poses for her portrait. All over the garden during the months of May and June there are these little pools of colour; and

24

though the sunlight gradually robs them of their lustre, so that they seem to fade into the ground on which they are resting, one can hardly feel sad about it. For the petals are only going home, returning to the good earth, under the sheltering arms of the mother who bore them.

We can now bring this chapter towards its conclusion with a list of those plants and shrubs in my own garden which *were* killed by the winter's rages. The list is not long but it is significant and sometimes surprising. It may have some value for those gardeners, at the beginning of their careers, who are misled by what they read in the nursery-men's catalogues or—more likely, since nurserymen are among the most honourable of men—may perversely ignore the warnings contained in them.

We will make out the list in alphabetical order, beginning with . . .

Azara microphylla. This is the rather rare and elegant little winter shrub whose praises I sang in *Garden Open Today.* We grow it for the sweet vanilla fragrance of its small white flowers, which normally begin to open in January. On sunny mornings there is something most exciting about this exotic scent drifting through the sharp crisp air. I have just been looking up what I wrote about this charmer. Here it is: 'The azara is not tough, nor is it unduly tender. The one essential is a wall, if possible a corner formed by two walls, because it is a wind-hater.'

It seems that this description was reasonably accurate. We planted two azaras, to be on the safe side, only a couple of feet away from each other. One of them gave up the ghost; the other, though it lost most of its leaves, broke out merrily

25

again in April. So next January, if you find yourself walking down Ham Gate Avenue, and are allured by an unexpected scent of vanilla, you will know where it comes from. And in your own garden you may think it worth gambling on its survival.

Ceanothus. We had two and a half varieties of ceanothus, of which only one survived. This enumeration is not perverse: the 'half' was rooted in the little front garden of my next-door neighbour, Mrs Poyser, but it had stretched its pretty arms so obligingly over my own plot that I had come to regard it as partly mine. (There should be more of this pleasing co-operation between neighbours.) This lovely old shrub was blasted to death by the icy winds that swept across the common, so if you are ordering a ceanothus I should cross this one off your list unless you have a very sheltered corner. It goes by the name of *Ceanothus dentatus.*

Another name to cross off, even if you *have* a sheltered corner, is *Ceanothus x Burkwoodii.* My own *x Burkwoodii* had one of the most cosseted corners in the whole garden, but it expired, swiftly and finally.

Which leaves us with . . . *Ceanothus* Autumnal Blue. This greeted the spring mornings with every appearance of a floral hangover, although it had the protection of a wall. But as the year advanced the vigour of its growth proved that it had emerged triumphant from an ordeal which, in all probability, it will never be called upon to endure again. Yes—Autumnal Blue is certainly your best bet.

Cryptomeria japonica elegans. This is the lovely conifer whose feathery foliage catches fire in the autumn so fiercely that you feel you can warm your hands over it. I was under the impression that it was tough; obviously it isn't. The winter put the fire out and killed it stone-dead. All the same, I

26

believe that with a minimum of protection it would survive.

The behaviour of *all* the conifers was somewhat unexpected. Some of the Lawson cypresses, which one had imagined to be as tough as guardsmen, looked scorched and miserable until the summer was well advanced, while the more aristocratic golden cypresses—*Chamaecyparis Lawsoniana lutea*—emerged comparatively unscathed.

Escallonia. Only the Irish, I am beginning to think, can grow escallonias to perfection. Whether the Irish deserve them is another matter; one can never make up one's mind, as one reads history, about what these bewildering, paradoxical, unpredictable and adorable people really do deserve. One can only affirm that what they deserve they never get, and what they don't deserve they do. Once, in another opus,[1] I observed that 'women, elephants and the Irish never forget an injury'. To this profound observation I would now append—'nor do escallonias'.

My own escallonias, certainly, never forgot the injury of the drastic winter with which this chapter is concerned. If I had the space I might here indulge in some fanciful analogies between horticulture and history; the particular escallonias of which I am writing hailed from Irish nurseries; and their conduct was almost excessively Irish. When one thought that they were dead they suddenly produced a leaf of shamrock green, and a flower as flaunting as a flag; and then, when one went to give them assistance, with the most amiable intentions, the flowers faded and the leaves withered. Though I say it myself, the long-drawn-out love-hate relationship between the British and the Irish could scarcely be more aptly summarized.

The only escallonia which British gardeners can grow with

[1] *The Sweet and Twenties* (London: Weidenfeld and Nicolson, 1960).

assurance is the hybrid *Escallonia x langleyensis*. This may not have quite the grace, nor the rosy bloom, nor the subtlety of my Irish varieties, which are dead and gone. But it stands up to the wind and the weather, and it is reasonably predictable.

Pieris formosa Forrestii. This—alas—succumbed.

Before writing more I will describe it, so that you may see why we indulged in the 'alas'! Nothing is more annoying than reading about things that one cannot visualize.

This pieris is one of the most spectacular examples in Nature of the triumph of the leaf over the flower. Now that I come to think of it, I cannot even remember what sort of flower it produces. But the leaves are lambent and luminous, and among the most magical of the many lanterns that are lit by April in the woods. If you live near London, and take yourself to the Isabella Plantation in Richmond Park, you can see these little lanterns glowing, lighting up the most dismal afternoon. The top leaves are of brilliant cherry red, faintly tinged with cinnamon, and they stay that colour for weeks on end, looking so festive that many people suppose them to be flowers. But they are obviously too frail for such assaults as they were asked to endure. All the same, I am ordering another one, and I shall provide it with a Polythene overcoat or, better still, a small tent.

Rosemary. The almost universal collapse of the rosemaries, throughout the British Isles, was one of the most painful, and one of the most startling, phenomena of the winter. One had somehow assumed that rosemaries were as tough as lavenders, maybe because one had so many memories of them in cottage gardens, where they grow to hedges four and five feet high. In *Garden Open Today* I celebrated the rosemaries at some length, mentioning several comparatively uncommon varieties which had given me special pleasure, notably, *Rosmarinus officinalis albus*, *Rosmarinus officinalis rosea*, and *Rosmarinus officinalis* Tuscan Blue. In self-defence, with regard to the last-named, I wrote, 'This is too tender for my liking.' But I imagined that the other two would weather the storms of a severe winter. Evidently they won't. So if you have a love of rosemaries you had best confine yourself to the old-fashioned favourite, *Rosmarinus officinalis angustifolius*. Even this variety, in my garden, was cut down to the ground. However, the roots survived.

Before we leave the rosemaries, may I call your attention to the charming origin of its name? My informant, as usual, was my old friend Marius, with his encyclopaedic erudition. I had always imagined that the name must be connected with some sort of sixteenth-century female, vaguely Shakespearean, who was in the habit of wandering through cottage gardens, permanently attired in a white apron, whisking sprays of rosemary into her olde-worlde basket. Not at all. The ancestry is from the Latin *ros*, which means spray, on account of its liking to grow over the cliffs of the Mediterranean, and *marinus*, which of course means sea. This sort of information, if dropped casually as you are walking round the garden, is calculated to irritate one's dearest friends.

This concludes our list of casualties, with the exception of a very few unfortunates in the cold greenhouse, to which we shall be referring in a moment. The reader may agree that we did pretty well, all things considered, and I fancy that this was the general experience in most of the gardens of the British Isles.

The Cold Greenhouse

The cold greenhouse was certainly cold, but not as cold

as we had feared. We have already noted on an earlier page that Mr Gaskin had difficulty in digging his way out to it through the snow drifts, and the only artificial heat it ever had was provided by a small cheap oil-stove which burned less than a gallon and a half of paraffin per week. In spite of this, the lowest temperature recorded throughout the winter was a mere two degrees of frost. When we remember that for days on end the surrounding countryside was near to zero point, and that the frail panes were constantly assaulted by a succession of ferocious blizzards, we may feel entitled to congratulate ourselves on this remarkable result. Some readers, indeed, may be inclined to suspect that it is almost too remarkable to be true.

But it is quite true. The secret of our success, which cut our casualties down to a minimum—a few scented-leaved species of pelargonium, an agapanthus and an abutilon—is contained in a single word, Polythene, with which Mr Page in his wisdom had draped the interior of the greenhouse earlier in the year. I have had some rude things to say about Polythene when it is used in the creation of ponds, because in this connection it evokes a strong suggestion of damp underwear—very old gentlemen's drawers, wringing wet. So let us now praise its virtues in the greenhouse. As an insulator against both heat and cold it is quite invaluable; without its protection the temperature would have dropped a further ten degrees. (This was in fact what happened in the unpolythened greenhouse of a neighbour of mine, in precisely similar conditions.) It is not exactly pretty but it is not unsightly and the vigour of my own plants suggests that it certainly does not shut out any vital light rays. The only possible objection to its use is that sometimes bumble-bees get under it, and work themselves into a frenzy. If they

do, you just have to pull out one of the drawing-pins and
shoo them away again, which is really not such a Herculean
undertaking.

One final word, about the lily-pond. Water, as you may
have gathered, is the foundation of my gardening philosophy.

*None of the water plants in the lily-pond were in the smallest
degree affected by the exceptional outrages of the season.*

(This really is one of the occasions when a writer can be
forgiven for indulging in italics.)

The roots of these exquisite things were encased in solid
ice for months on end. Were they perturbed? In no degree.
Came April, and the golden rosettes of the calthas, double
marsh-marigolds, shone more brightly than ever; came May
and the slim spears of the *Iris laevigata* were lifted high, and
the petals of their Dresden china blossoms were already
unfolding. By early summer the water lilies—*Laydekeri* and
Albatross—were spreading themselves in a profusion of pink
and white; and in August the pontederias, with their leaves
like thrusting fingers, were giving a sparkling display of
hyacinth-blue. Of all the battles in the garden, which the
flowers fought and won, the battle of the lily-pond was the
bravest and the most brilliant.

PRACTICAL NOTE

This might be a good place to say a word about cloches.
I am not 'agin' them, but they have some disadvantages and
limitations. The glass variety inevitably get broken, sooner
or later, and one finds oneself landed with a lot of twisted
wire and splintered panes, which will certainly cause scowls
and mutterings on Tuesday afternoons, when the dustmen
call. And the plastic cloches have a habit of blowing away
in a high wind. But perhaps the most boring thing about

cloches is that they don't fit into odd corners. If you are permanently dedicated to growing interminable rows of early lettuces in long straight lines, cloches are obviously your best bet. But if, like most amateur gardeners, you have to deal with small irregular patches, such as an awkward triangle of tender rosemaries, recently planted out, you will begin to wonder if cloches may not be more bother than they are worth.

This is where we introduce Mr Page's Polythene Invention, which could not be simpler, cheaper, or more effective. This is all that we need to do. Gather a bunch of bracken, spread it thickly over the plant or the patch of earth which we wish to protect, cut out a piece of Polythene to match, place it over the bracken, and pin it securely to the ground with two or three bricks. If no bracken is available, a bucketful of dead leaves will do as well. Obviously, we cannot employ this technique to protect tall plants, but for short ones, or for delicate bulbs, such as crinum, amaryllis or the family of agapanthus, it is invaluable. The Polythene forms a sort of miniature tent which is almost as effective as a cold greenhouse and far less unsightly than a cloche. During exceptionally dry spells, or on specially sunny days when winter is drawing to a close, we can lift up the Polythene and give a sprinkling of water.

For this and, as we shall see, for numerous other devices of equal ingenuity, Mr Page, it will be generally agreed, deserves the gratitude of mankind.

CHAPTER TWO

THE WAY YOU LOOK AT IT

Scene

The porch of the music-room. Through the windows one can see a moonlit lawn, still faintly streaked with snow.

Time

The small hours of a bitter morning in March.

Dramatis Personae

Gaskin, in his accustomed role of factotum.
Four and Five, in their accustomed mood of *hauteur* and disdain, which they never fail to display when I return home

33

after a long absence. Both are sitting very close to the fire with their backs squarely turned towards me. From time to time they glance at one another with meaningful expressions. 'This sort of thing,' they are saying, 'is becoming far too frequent. He seems to imagine that he can go away for months on end and then expect us to behave as though nothing had happened. He must not be allowed to get away with it. He must be *shown*.' And show me they do, in the most unmistakable manner. It will be nearly a week before they really relax.

Finally myself, a little dazed after jetting across the Atlantic, but itching to get into the garden in spite of the fact that it would really be more sensible to wait till dawn.

So I say good night and Gaskin picks up Four and Five in a single accomplished swoop. They dangle in front of him, a most alluring bundle of scorched fur, faintly powdered with wood-ash. I step towards them hoping that they will at least show some sign of recognition. I am greeted by two green, icy stares. I should have known better.

And now we can open the door of the porch and step outside.

In the bright moonlight the garden was like the setting for a winter ballet when the stage is deserted, the dancers have gone home, and the music has echoed into silence. But even now there was a faint music, for a thaw was setting in, and from underneath the branches of the copper beech came a ghostly tinkle of sharps and trebles, as the drops fell gently on to the frozen leaves. By noon tomorrow most of the snow would have gone.

And yet, over in the distance, there was still a thick drift of it, dazzling white beneath the moon. I wondered why it had stayed there; maybe because of the lie of the land, or because Page had been protecting something with a wattle fence. I stepped over to investigate, and then, as I drew closer, I saw that this whiteness was not the whiteness of snow but of blossom. The whole bank was ablaze with winter heather, flowering as it had never flowered before.

This was a great moment in my gardening life, for there could have been no more vivid vindication of one's constant praises of the exquisite little plant—*Erica carnea* Springwood White. Years ago, in another book, and in the first flush of enthusiasm, I wrote that it would grow on an iceberg. Well, this was precisely what it had been doing. As I bent down, flashing the torch for a closer inspection, the blossoms showed themselves to be immaculate, untouched by the faintest stain of brown. They might have been spending the winter snugly enclosed within a glass case.

Side by side with the whites, only now coming into view as the torch flashed over them, were the pinks, *Erica carnea* King George, fresh and rosy and equally unaffected by the winter's rages. If there had been no other flowers in the garden, it would still have been a place of gaiety and festival.

This is the last time that I shall write about the winter heathers because if people do not grow them after this dramatic and strictly factual exposition of their virtues they had better stay indoors, and spend the rest of their lives wiping the dust off their wax begonias. But since we have stumbled upon them in this exciting manner I shall pause for a practical note, about heathers in general, because perhaps there is something to be said about them that has not been said before.

35

PRACTICAL NOTE

Heathers. The Psychological Approach. You may well enquire what is meant by the 'psychological approach'. I can best explain this by asking you to consider the garden of a neighbour of mine, the late Dowager Lady Linlithgow, who used to live on the other side of the common. In her garden there was not a single sprig of heather. Why? Not because she did not love it but because she loved it too much. Heather, to her, meant Scotland; it meant the hills and valleys that she knew so well at her old home, Hopetoun, which is perhaps the most lyrically beautiful building in the British Isles. The one thing that heather did *not* mean was a patch of colour in a small, or comparatively small, provincial garden. It would have been as out of place as the portrait of an enormous and empurpled ancestor hanging in the spare bedroom of a maisonette.

What has all this got to do with the average gardener, who is unlikely to have a stately home in the background of his life, and has therefore no cause for these prejudices? In my opinion, quite a lot. I believe that many people are, as it were, 'psychologically conditioned' against certain flowers, and that this is a factor which should be taken into serious account by the writer on practical gardening.

Consider the Strange Case of John Betjeman and the Rhododendrons. One of the few reasons for hoping that the entire population of Britain is not nuts is the popularity of John Betjeman's poetry. A hundred thousand copies were sold of *A Few Late Chrysanthemums* and it is very comforting to think of those clean, sweet verses making themselves heard through the national discord. John, one would have thought, had the innocence of eye which would have reflected beauty without any irrelevant associations, and yet, when confronted by a rhododendron, he does not see a rhododendron; he sees a stockbroker. He is blind to all those brilliant carnival colours, the carmines and the cherries and the purples and the lemon yellows, because always in the background he sees a bogus Tudor mansion and snuffs the acrid aroma of cigar smoke. And he is not the only one. There are hundreds of people who share this strange obsession that all rhododendrons are 'stockbrokers' flowers', just as there are hundreds of people who feel that all orchids are 'evil'. If you doubt this, take a walk through the Orchid House at Kew and listen to the comments of the idiotic visitors, which are mostly on the lines of 'Ooo . . . er, it fair gives me the creeps'!

Back to the heathers. I believe that the reason why so few people realize the unlimited possibilities of the great heather family lies in the fact that they have so often seen them planted in a manner which outrages their natural inclinations—in formal beds, or in feeble little clumps of half a dozen, or lined like soldiers against a brick wall. No other plants in nature more bitterly resent a formal treatment; but no other plants more generously repay a sympathetic understanding.

Here are my own rules for growing heathers. If they sound arbitrary, I cannot help it. They have proved very successful indeed.

1. *Obey the dictates of the soil.* If there is much lime in your garden the number of species that you can grow will be limited, but you will still be able to avail yourself of *all* the winter-flowering varieties of carnea, and there are no less than twenty-five of these. Moreover, 'winter-flowering' in this case has a very wide interpretation, ranging from mid-

November to early April. Again, in some cases the beauty of the flowers themselves is equalled, if not surpassed, by the beauty of the foliage. A clump of *Erica carnea aurea* has foliage of such brilliant gold that soon after Christmas it gives the illusion of sunlight on the lawn.

Again, in quite limy soils you can succeed with most of the Mediterranean heaths, which will give you colour in spring and height all the year round. The comparatively common *Erica mediterranea*, for example, reaches a height of five feet, and its pink blossoms shine brightly against the dark green foliage. There are at least a dozen Mediterranean heaths to choose from, in whites and pinks, ranging from two to six feet, and flowering well into June.

The only other heather which you can safely plant in a chalky soil is the Corsican heath, *Erica terminalis*, which flowers in July. Although my favourite heather-firm describes this as 'forming well-shaped bushes', my experience does not bear this out. My own Corsican heaths have always looked rather raffish and swashbuckling.

The owners of gardens with only a faint trace of lime might experiment with the beautiful midsummer *Erica vagans*, particularly if they take the trouble to treat it with occasional doses of Sequestrene, the admirable product which in a previous book I described as 'God's gift to those who live on soils impregnated with chalk'. It will not perform miracles but it counteracts, say, twenty per cent of alkalinity.

On acid soils, the list of heathers is greatly extended. Some of these are mentioned in the appendix.

2. *Plant your heathers in splodges.* You are standing in the middle of a square empty lawn, determined to have a heather garden but wondering how on earth you can make it look natural, as though it had arrived there of its own

accord. This really *is* a problem, as I discovered when I began. After endless prowlings, mutterings, stickings-in of bamboo stakes, coupled with a great deal of squintings and neck-crickings and even bendings-double to see how it looked upside down through one's legs, I arrived at what seems to me the only solution, which is to make a 'splodge', almost as if you were making a big blot of ink on a sheet of paper. This may sound something of an anti-climax. But splodges—really vital and significant splodges—are not all that easy to make. This, presumably, would also be the excuse of a breed of artists for whom I have no great fondness, the 'action' painters, who create their masterpieces by hurling fistfuls of paint across the room at an empty canvas. (Judging by my few social contacts with these persons and their mistresses the paint sometimes seems to have gone astray and landed on the mistresses.) However, in this particular connection I believe that the action painters have really 'got something'.

When you are making your splodge be sure that you make it big enough. If you are going in for heathers, an aerial view of your garden should show them up like a small lake of colour in a green island. If you can only afford the money or the space for half a dozen you had better forget about them—to your eternal regret.

Still on the question of design, we come to our third principle . . .

3. *Always plant heathers on a slope.* Or—at least—contrive the *illusion* of a slope. In our own case this was achieved by digging a hole in the lawn to make a pond, emptying the earth on to the adjoining grass, bouncing ourselves about on the ensuing mound to get it into shape, and then stepping back, squinting at it sideways, and 'psychologically adjust-

ing ourselves'. By these processes we found ourselves in possession of a small hill, all ready for planting with heather. Or thought we did, which is much the same thing.

If you do not want to dig a pond, you will just have to get the earth from some other part of the garden. If the worst comes to the worst you will have to put a sack in the boot of the car and scrape it up from lonely lanes during the weekends, feeling like Crippen as you do so. After all, there is a great deal of earth in the world and it is just too weak and silly to say that you cannot go and get some of it. People who make such excuses are not worthy to be called gardeners.

This 'illusion of a slope' can be enhanced if at the top of your little hill, even if it is only a foot higher than the rest of the ground, you plant something like a slow-growing silver cypress *Chamaecyparis Lawsoniana Fletcheri*, which will stick up like the spire of a steeple, and at the bottom something like a prostrate cotoneaster which will 'pull your eye down'.

All this will take a lot of trouble and it will make a great deal of mess, so it is not to be recommended to persons who are plunged into gloom if one of their standard roses is planted an inch too near its neighbour. But if you are one of those to whom a garden is a place for shaping a little world of your own according to your heart's desire, it will give you many hours of great happiness.

4. *Confine yourself to a few varieties grouped in mass.* Do not plant six of one and half a dozen of the other. My own scheme might serve as a working model. Here it is:

Two broad irregular bands of winter heather, one white and one pink. These are in full flower from early December till the end of March, tight, closely packed blossom, weed-proof, fool-proof, weather-proof.

Next, a wide curving 'splodge' of *Erica vagans* Mrs D. F. Maxwell which is a mass of rosy pink through July, August and September. After this the flowers go a rich brown, when they are perhaps even more beautiful.

Finally, a rather unexpected intrusion of a clump of *Erica Tetralix* such as you might find on a natural moorland where there is a sudden freak patch of damper soil. This is the heather which makes such an exquisite tinkle when you kneel beside it and flick the flower-bells.

So much for the main group, which is bang in the centre of the garden in full sunlight. Here and there round my small domain there are other heathers, such as a cluster of the magically beautiful Irish bog heather *Daboecia cantabrica*, which flowers in semi-shade, and a very gallant trio of the tall tree heathers, *Erica arborea alpina*, which really should be awarded some sort of floral V.C. for the way in which they stood up to the assaults of that winter. Although the feathery branches were bent right to the ground by the snow, and nailed there by the ice for weeks on end, they straightened themselves in the first sunshine and by the end of April they were so starred with blossom that the bees never left them alone.

Pause for a Thought about Bees. I have always been mystified by the strange behaviour of bees who keep on bumbling into flowers that must obviously have been drained dry of honey, or pollen, or whatever it is that bees are going after. If you have an hour to spare on a summer afternoon, sit on the lawn in front of a cluster of Canterbury Bells and you will see what I mean. Enter a bee. It plunges into the heart of one of the bells and stays there for quite a long time, waving its behind at you in a state of obvious ecstasy. Then it gets out, looking faintly tight, and bumbles off to another flower. And that, you say to yourself, is that. Obviously there can't be much honey left in *that* particular blossom; the till has been robbed and the cupboard is bare. But no. For now along comes another bee, to plunge into the same bell and to stay there just as long, with its behind going up and down in even more ecstatic rhythms. What is happening? Why these curious convulsions? Bee after bee, behind after behind —and so it goes on through the long drowsy afternoon. Not for the first time one wishes that Darwin was by one's side to explain it all.

Whatever the explanation, it would doubtless be strange and beautiful and in tune with the mysterious rhythms of the wind on the meadow.

Heathers, as the reader may have opined, go to my head. So let us try to make the rest of this chapter as grimly factual as an engineering prospectus. (Though, as it happens, the only engineering prospectus I ever read was written in such purple prose that it was almost embarrassing. So were the photographs, portraying enormous square-shouldered engineers, standing by their bridges and their pylons, with their wives fluttering in the background. The engineers were gazing at their gaunt, skeletal creations with such obvious ecstasy that they seemed to be longing to commit some sort of mechanical adultery.)

The most important fact to note is that of all the gardens that can be conceived or brought into existence, a heather garden is by far the cheapest. There are two reasons for this, and the first is concerned with labour. Once a heather garden is established there is nothing to be done but sit down and enjoy it or—if we are in a sportive mood— to lie down and roll on it. There is no need to water, nor clip, nor protect, nor cosset it in any way whatsoever; above all, unless we are exceptionally unlucky, there is no need to weed it. My own heather beds, after five years, are now so tightly packed with flower and foliage that you could not find a weed in them if you were to search for weeks.

What do we mean by 'unless we are exceptionally unlucky'? Well, there is one weed—as far as I am aware, the only one—with which heathers cannot cope of their own accord. This is the 'dodder', *Cuscuta epithymum*, and the very devil it is. The dodder defeats the heathers because it is a total parasite, so that they have no chance to smother it. It looks like threads of red cotton and since it bears no leaves you may not know that it has arrived until it begins to produce its small pinkish flowers. Even then, you may not realize what you are in for; you may think that it is just a pretty little wild thing that can be pulled out if it becomes too intrusive. Only when whole plants begin to turn a sickly yellow will you wake up to the fact that there is a killer in your midst.

This is what happened in one of my own gardens, and it took months of painful experiment to defeat it. I began by snipping away dozens of infected growths with a pair of nail scissors, and ended with digging out whole plants. Still the wretched thing persisted; it seemed indestructible. In despair I sought the help of the R.H.S. Gardens at Wisley and together we tried an experiment. In some recent tests on lawns, so they told me, heather had proved fully resistant to certain selective weed-killers such as Verdone, while dodder had proved only partly resistant. Might it not therefore be possible that if the weed-killer were used at double strength it would kill the dodder without killing the heather?

The thought of deluging a beloved bed of heathers with double-strength weed-killer was not appealing but there seemed to be no alternative, so we took the risk. For several months afterwards the heathers looked on the point of death but they eventually recovered. And the dodder was killed for good and all.

Moral—when they arrive from the nurserymen, always examine your heathers very carefully for that tell-tale cotton-like thread. No reputable firm would deliberately send you infected plants but the dodder is so cunning and so persistent that it sometimes manages to creep into the most respectable circles.

The second reason why a heather garden is—or can be—the cheapest garden in the world is because of the ease with which you can increase it, either by taking cuttings or by layering. In five years my own bed of white winter heather, which began with twelve small specimens planted two feet apart, has layered itself at such a pace that it is now a mass of solid blossom spreading over an area roughly ten times larger than the original plantation. If we were so inclined we could let it rip till it covered the whole lawn. But this would mean that there would be no work left for Mr Page to do, which, as the reader will agree, would be tantamount to a national disaster. So next year I shall have to begin giving clumps of it away, preferably to persons with limited means but unlimited numbers of cats. For, as a final practical note, I seem to have omitted to mention that well-established clumps of heather are in great favour with equally well-established felines, who like to lie in it, dabbing at the bees and pretending to be lions.

CHAPTER THREE

THIS BLESSED PLOT

THE wide sale of John Betjeman's poetry—so we suggested in the previous chapter—is a cause for optimism when we survey the national scene. There must be traces of sanity left in us when we can respond, not only to the music of his songs of the flowers and the fields, but also to the anguish with which he contemplates their destruction . . .

Cut down that timber! Bells too many and strong
Pouring their music through the branches bare
From moon-white churches down the windy air
Have pealed the centuries out with Evensong.

Remove those cottages, a huddled throng!
Too many babies have been born in there,
Too many coffins, bumping down the stair,
Carried the old their garden paths along . . .[1]

If we look around us with eyes that are not too jaundiced we may perhaps detect other hopeful signs. Among these the most unexpected is the popularity of the stately homes of England and the gardens in which they stand. In the past decade these places—so exquisitely anachronistic in the Welfare State—have attracted such immense crowds that they must now be regarded as an important factor in the entertainment industry.

Admittedly, their appeal is not always primarily aesthetic. Lord Montagu of Beaulieu, for example, would be the first to admit that for every person who pays to see his daffodils at least two pay to see his Daimlers. These ancient horrors, these hideous precursors of the machine age, have an almost morbid attraction for the ton-up generation; to watch a bunch of youths staring at them, even attempting to fondle them, is to be reminded of a group of stage-struck juveniles conjuring up erotic fantasies about elderly actresses. Again, when the turnstiles tinkle at the Duke of Bedford's Woburn Abbey, the number of people who are eager to study the Canalettos is probably less than the number of people who are eager to study the duke.

None the less, though their motives may be suspect, the holiday crowds must absorb some of the atmosphere even if they do so unconsciously, as they wander through the great halls and up the winding staircases. After several hours with the masterpieces of Chippendale they may have doubts

[1] From 'The Planster's Vision' in *Collected Poems* by John Betjeman (London: John Murray, 1958). By kind permission of the publishers.

46

about their chromium-plated commodes. As for the gardens, they will surely see flowers that they have never seen before, and they may well be so attracted by these flowers that they will bend down to read the labels. Sometimes they may even remember the names on the labels and order the flowers for their own modest plots.

We can now come more closely to the subject of this chapter. The gardens which, to my mind, have the most magical 'atmosphere' in the British Isles—and some of the most exciting labels—are the Savill Gardens at Windsor Great Park. And the astonishing thing is that the great majority of the British public never seem even to have heard of them. They swarm like ants over the lawns at Kew, they crowd the paths at Wisley, but in the Savill Gardens you may often wander around for hours without meeting more than a handful of people. I have been doing this most blissfully for years, and it is therefore a very Christian act to entreat large numbers of people to intrude upon this solitude.

However, the entreaty must be made, because if we are ever going to attain to any sort of mastery in this art of gardening we *must* get out and about, we *must* see what is happening in the world around us. Surely this applies to every art, minor or major? She would indeed be a dull cook who never moved out of her own kitchen.

The Savill Gardens are within very easy access of London. What follows is for those who for various reasons beyond their control are unable to visit them in person.

When I first saw Sir Eric Savill, standing in the doorway of his exceptionally pretty house in Windsor Great Park, with the giant oaks and beeches of the Savill Gardens brooding in the distance behind him, I said to myself, 'Where have I seen that face before?'

Then I remembered. Sir Nathaniel Dance's portrait of Capability Brown, which hangs in a corner of one of the state rooms of Burleigh House. The features are not identical but the feeling of kinship is remarkable. Even if you had not read the label on the picture, nor been introduced to the man in the doorway, you would have known instinctively that they were both men of the open air, men of humour, and men of taste—though perhaps that is too pale a word. Men, shall we say, of sturdy elegance.

I have always had a special fondness for Capability Brown, maybe because in all the many lovely landscapes which he brought into being, his mind seems to have marched in step with my own and his eye seems to have seen what I might have seen myself. 'Yes—he *had* to contrive that little hill, and it was inevitable that he should have planted that avenue precisely where he planted it, and of course that lake could be nowhere else—it completes the design with a single silver gesture.' The fact that one has this impression is probably only an indirect tribute to his art; if one had been in his place one might well have made a botch of it. All the same, it is pleasant to wander through landscapes where one wants to alter hardly anything, and where one feels that Nature has been gently but firmly put in her proper place. Especially am I conscious of this in my daily walks through Richmond Park. Although Capability Brown's successors have done their best to destroy his handiwork the general harmony of the design persists, and his giant oaks continue to laud his memory. (When I was in America, at a time when General de Gaulle was spitting his synthetic Napoleonic venom at the British, I experienced a certain acid satisfaction in reminding my audiences that those oaks had been planted some fifty years before the first of the many French revolutions and would most certainly be standing fifty years after the next one—which might be sooner than we expected.)

I have introduced the Savill Gardens with the portrait of a man because that is precisely what they are—the portrait of a man. Unlike any public gardens in the British Isles they bear the stamp of a single signature.[1] The canvas on which the portrait was to be painted dates from 1931 when young Savill was appointed Deputy Surveyor of Windsor Park and Woods. At that time, incredible as it may seem, there was no garden of any sort in the whole of the Great Park. It was not till the advent of George V and Queen Mary that down in the forest something stirred. Even then, it might not have stirred if young Savill, in the course of his duties, had not been prowling about among the ponticums, pushing his way through the brambles, and saying to himself—as the Duke of Windsor said, on another historic occasion—'Something must be done.'

And something *was* done, in the winter of 1932—something small but something exciting. After eighteen months of prowling and pushing young Savill stopped dead in his tracks, in the centre of the jungle, and said to himself, 'Here it is. This is where we start.' He was up to the neck in wild rhododendrons, laurels, elders and bracken. There was enough wild life around him, in the shape of rabbits, hares and deer, to equip a Disney super-feature. But the soil was

---

[1] The serious student of these gardens, who wishes to acquaint himself with their history and the long catalogue of their treasures, must be referred to *The Gardens in the Royal Park at Windsor* by Lanning Roper, published by Chatto & Windus.

rich and vibrant, there was the distant tinkle of streams, and there were giant trees with sheltering arms. There was, in short, the beginning of a garden, and he knew that he was the man to make it. On that cold morning, thirty years ago, he must have been a very happy man, and I only wish that I had been standing by his side.

This may not be history as it should be written, but it is the only sort of history that I can write and, incidentally, the only sort of history that I care to read. However, perhaps we had better pin down these fluttering pages with a date and a royal anecdote. The date is April 14, 1934. By then, the first stages in the conquest of the jungle had been completed. Rides had been opened, ditches had been cleared, trees had been felled, and pools of water were broadening into potential lakes. (Not for the first time, and certainly not for the last, I take this opportunity of reminding the reader that *every* garden must begin with water in some shape or form even if it is only a pool two feet square sunk into a little concrete terrace. If the reader's retort is, 'In that case, I haven't got a garden at all because I haven't got any water in it,' my reply is, 'Quite. You haven't got a garden.')

Back to our date and our royal anecdote. April 14, 1934. Enter George and Mary, threading their way down the sylvan glades. The pen of Mr Lanning Roper, author of the aforesaid scholarly work on the Royal Gardens, is normally so discreetly disciplined and conducted that we cannot imagine it betraying him into any indiscretions. But on this occasion the drama of the situation gives this pen a lively twitch. For it seems that Queen Mary, on nearing the centre of the stage, scraped her immortal toque on the branches of an overhanging *Quercus Ilex*. God alone knows what might have happened if the scrape had been more severe, for only

God can make a tree, and—as Queen Mary was well aware—
only God can make a Queen. But the toque remained intact,
and the bough swung back into position. The Queen, with
her shrewd blue eyes, looked around her. Then she turned
to young Savill, with the smile that still lightens the pages
of British history, and she said: 'It's very nice, Mr Savill,
but isn't it rather small?'

I cannot better Mr Lanning Roper's comment on these
gentle but potentially explosive words. He writes: 'This was
the longed-for accolade; this was the green light.'

In short, this was the birth of the Savill Gardens.

Some titles come to an author after hours of thought, and
sweat, and wrestling with his soul and with his publishers.
Other titles write themselves swiftly, almost automatically,
as soon as he sets pen to paper—such as the title of the
present chapter, 'This Blessed Plot'.

As soon as I had written those words I turned to *King
Richard II*, Act II, Scene 1, to see if they fitted as well as I
suspected. They did. Shakespeare, quite obviously, had been
writing, by some strange telekinetic process of the subconscious, about the Savill Gardens. 'This royal throne of
kings'—there is a noble rise in the Valley Garden, sur-
mounted by a single majestic oak—'this sceptred isle . . .'
And round the lake the lilies rise as proudly as sceptres.

> This other Eden, demi-paradise,
> This fortress built by Nature for herself
> Against infection and the hand of war . . .

Is the parallel far-fetched? I think not. The gardens are
as near to the Garden of Eden as we are likely to get in this

wicked world; at all times of the year they are a demi-paradise and at some times of the year you can cross out the 'demi'; and they are certainly a 'fortress built by Nature for herself'.

One of the miracles of the Savill Gardens is the lie of the land. The gardener's greatest enemy is wind. Not frost, nor snow, nor drought, nor even the sullen implacability of the soil, but wind—the wind that claws and rips at root and branch. In these gardens the wind, if not actually defeated, is kept at bay by the rise and fall of the land, and by the giant bastions of trees that have endured the assaults of centuries of cruel weather.

I am now going to suggest a few reasons why Mr and Mrs Smith, owners of half an acre in a suburb of Wimbledon, should visit these gardens, and how they might profit from doing so.

` The first reason can be summed up in a single word—seed. As soon as one has walked through the main gate, and through the little gate beside the lake, over whose waters the trees are hung like a giant Gobelin tapestry, one begins to be dramatically reminded of one of the basic miracles not only of gardening but of life itself, the miracle of seed, and of seedlings gathering round the parent plants in the rich earth—I almost wrote 'dancing' round them, for there is a sort of joyous luxuriance about the whole process. Only too often flowers come to us second-hand, through the pages of a catalogue via the parcel post, in boxes of bulbs in cellophane bags, or wrapped in sacking at the back of a lorry. Even when we are sowing seed in our own gardens we must first break open the packet in which they are contained, where they have been sleeping for months. And the 'miracle', thereby, is ever so faintly dimmed.

But at the Savill Gardens there is none of this. You wander down a winding path, your eye is caught by a cluster of primulas, you bend down to examine it, and you suddenly notice that the earth all round is dotted with hundreds of tiny primula seedlings, clustering round the parent plant like chickens round a hen.

Your reaction will vary according to your temperament. You may say to yourself—particularly if the primula is of a rare and exquisite variety—'Surely they would not miss just *one* of these seedlings if I bent down and scooped it up?' You may even glance over your shoulder to see if you are being observed . . . and there it would be wise to put the thought aside, for even at the Savill Gardens, in glades that are apparently deserted, hawk-eyed young gentlemen have a habit of popping out of the undergrowth.

Or you may say to yourself, with some tetchiness, 'How is it that there are *only* primula seedlings round the parent plant? Why are they not struggling, as they would be in my own garden, with docks and dandelions and bindweed and oxalis? What magic potions do these people use?' The answer is something of an anti-climax. There are no magic potions. There is nothing but the fingers of the aforesaid hawk-eyed young gentlemen, tirelessly weeding by hand. I find this refreshing. In this day and age, when we are inclined to rely more and more upon the efforts of robots in various shapes and guises, it is salutary to be reminded that there are still some tasks for which human fingers are indispensable. One of the most popular slogans in the advertising world, when a gadget is being promoted, is that it 'takes the backache out of' whatever chore may be involved. But backache is an essential ingredient of success in all the arts, and not only the art of gardening. I doubt if you can even take the backache out of the art of love.

Let us illustrate this with a practical example. If you go to the Savill Gardens in early spring one of the most ravishing spectacles is provided by the hosts of miniature daffodils, shimmering in golden pools under the leafless trees, tumbling in a medley of yellows down the banks, or preening themselves by the side of a winding stream. As my pen is obviously straying very near to the purple ink-pot, let us hasten to check it by observing that the four main components of these groups are formed by the following species:

Narcissus cyclamineus. This is perhaps the most beautiful of all, because of the design of its tiny flowers, whose petals— as its name implies—are bent back like those of a cyclamen.

Narcissus asturiensis. I would put this second because of the buttercup brilliance of its gold.

Narcissus Bulbocodium citrinus and *Narcissus triandrus albus.* Both these are paler varieties, and Mr Page thinks that they are the most beautiful. We will not quarrel with him. It is foolish to try to place them in any order of merit when they are all so lovely.

All this golden host is self-sown from a few dozen original bulbs. Whereupon Mr and Mrs Smith, and ten thousand owners of other suburban plots, may remind me that *they* have not got woodland banks and open meadows and winding streams and all the rest of it. They might even add that they have not got government grants, nor royal patronage, and that it is highly improbable that the shadow of the Queen Mother will ever fall across their garden paths.

They have a point there; but they have not quite got all the point. Like my imaginary critics, I have none of these advantages. However, I *have* got a cluster of two dozen *Narcissus cyclamineus* under a small tree on the lawn and up till now, when the grass has grown high in June, I have clipped it, daffodils and all. Henceforth I shall leave it, till the flowers have ripened and shed their seed, for this is what they do at the Savill Gardens, with the results which I have been attempting to describe. No doubt this small patch of lawn will look rather unkempt during the summer months, but I do not greatly care. For next spring, when I kneel down to greet the first small specks of gold from the flowers, maybe I shall see around them some spikes of delicate green that are not blades of grass but blades of seedling daffodils.

Now for a second reason for visiting the Savill Gardens. Again it can be summed up in a single word . . . colour. There is no garden in the world where colours are blended with greater skill and delicacy; indeed, in the entire acreage, throughout all the seasons of the year, I have only come across one scheme which seemed unfortunate. ('Unfortunate' is a mild description of the aversion I felt for it.) This was a group of brilliant yellow *Lysichitum americanum*—the American Skunk Cabbage—rising from a bed of shocking-pink *Primula rosea*. At first I thought that there must have been some mistake, and that some careless gardener had mixed up a box of seedlings. But no—this violent concatenation of colour is repeated at several points in the gardens; moreover it is 'starred', so that the flowers are visible from great distances, reflected in the water of the lake. I said to Sir Eric, politely but firmly, 'I don't like this at all.' To which he replied, politely but firmly, 'Well, I *do*.' And that was that. As we observed on an earlier page, this is one man's garden, and every twist and turn of it bears his signature.

I wonder what women would think of that colour scheme?

Now that we have asked that question, I can write something that has been on the tip of my pen for several pages. More than any other garden in the world the Savill garden is a woman's garden. To describe it as *only* a woman's would be, of course, ridiculous; what I mean is that it is a woman's garden in the sense that it will make an immediate appeal even to women who are totally disinterested in gardening *per se*, merely because of its brilliant and audacious use of colour. It is as though they were to wander for the first time into a vast new emporium where some original genius had been given a free hand in contriving colour schemes which nobody had ever thought of before.

Here are one or two examples:

1. A raised bed of purple thyme with *Tropaeolum polyphyllum* climbing over it. This is a particularly brilliant miniature yellow nasturtium with an orange centre. We shall have more to say about the nasturtium family in another chapter; in the meantime it is enough to say that this combination is a shock, a tonic, and a sheer delight.

2. The luminous blue of *Meconopsis grandis* towering over the uncompromising orange-red of *Primula chungensis*. The meconopsis is a giant edition of the commoner blue poppy, and of all the blues in nature it comes nearest to the blue in the stained glass of an old church window when the sun is shining through it. Sir Eric tells me that they grow like weeds provided that they are planted in semi-shade in a completely acid soil. Well, mine don't seem to be quite so accommodating, but I shall go on trying. And you should go on trying too, for though they are almost impossible to grow from seed they have the happy characteristic of developing numerous basal shoots, which makes them easily divisible.

3. Snowdrops growing among the marbled leaves of *Cyclamen*

neapolitanum at the base of a giant oak. Perhaps this can hardly be described as a 'colour scheme', though the moss on the bark and the stalks of the snowdrops and the leaves of the cyclamen are all in different shades of green. But I have never seen snowdrops look so exquisite before, and next time you are ordering them I should definitely order some cyclamen at the same time. They form the happiest marriage imaginable.

4. Several groups of white and red rhododendrons growing so closely together that the flowers might have been on the same tree. They were the white species *R. calophytum* and the red hybrid Cornish Cross. Odd as it may be, I had forgotten about white and red in close conjunction, though I do seem to remember how pretty they were in a bed of Sweet Williams the year before last. You may say that this, again, can hardly be regarded as a 'colour scheme'. I disagree. Anyway, it has given me some new ideas for doing up my little extra bedroom.

5. The Kurume Punch Bowl. This is almost impossible to describe; one might as well attempt a thumbnail sketch of the Grand Canyon. Indeed, on American visitors it has much the same effect as that monstrous natural extravaganza. For the Punch Bowl *is* a sort of Grand Canyon of colour—the colour being provided by literally tens of thousands of Kurume azaleas.[1] When you first come upon them in May, after walking through the Valley Garden under the green shadows of the larches, you feel as if you had suddenly stumbled upon a Niagara Falls in which the waters foam in torrents of scarlet and orange and pink and purple and white and vermilion. Mr and Mrs Smith, with

---

[1] They take their name from the city of Kurume in the southern Japanese island of Kyushu.

their half an acre, of which a large proportion has to be devoted to Brussels sprouts, may feel that such glories are hardly within their grasp. But even here a visit to the Savill Gardens has a practical application to most gardeners and to all women. For as they wander round the Punch Bowl they will be shocked—and entranced—by combinations of colour which will give them ideas for the decoration of their homes and the adornment of their persons.

So it goes on throughout the year, the garden glowing and sparkling, till the coloured waves of Michaelmas daisies shine through the mists of October in the herbaceous borders, and the leaves of the maples break into their scarlet flames, which flicker over the pale candles of the autumn crocuses clustering round their base. When winter comes the garden loses none of its magic, for now we can perceive the bare beauty of its bones and delight in the melodic line of its hills and valleys. And still there is colour; you will never see greens more vivid than the carpets of moss that Nature has spread under the beeches, nor whites more immaculate than the slender branches of the silver birches. If you persevere, and go on exploring, you may find—even on Christmas day—a sudden bonfire of scarlet, such as the group of *Rhododendron Jacksonii*, which nestles in the sheltered corner of the Valley Garden.

Now for the third reason for visiting the Savill Gardens. Again, a single word will cover it . . . design. It is possible that here Mr and Mrs Smith may have some genuine grounds for complaining that the various ways in which Sir Eric has treated his rolling acres of woodland and valley can have no possible application to their own half-acre.

And yet if they keep their eyes open they will observe that he has worked on certain principles which have—at any rate in my opinion—a universal application. Thus, they will notice that he has invariably planted in *odd numbers*. Three cherries, or five, or whatever the number may be, never two or four. I have always done this myself, instinctively, ever since I planted my first trees. Why? I suppose the answer lies in the fact that one has tried to walk with Nature, and that Nature does not dispose her treasures in squares or in parallel lines. Talking of walking with Nature brings us to the second principle on which Sir Eric has worked. When he has been in any doubt concerning—let us say—the curve of a path he has followed the natural inclination of his own footsteps, and the line he has traced has been right, not only to walk over but to look at. This really does have a practical application to the Mr and Mrs Smiths of this world, among whom I here include myself. On several occasions, while making a garden, I have tried to edge myself away, as it were, from the path along which my feet were carrying me, because I wanted to plant a tree in the middle of it, or to interrupt it with the extension of a bed of flowers. Always, in the end, I have found that my footsteps were guiding me aright. All the same there is no need to carry this principle to extremes; a straight diagonal line across the lawn from the porch to the greenhouse would not be aesthetically very rewarding. Which brings us to Sir Eric's last principle: no straight lines. In the whole vast armoury at Nature's disposal there is no such thing as a ruler. Which means, as far as Mr and Mrs Smith are concerned, that the only border in the garden which should ever be straight is one which runs parallel with the house, and which can therefore be regarded with the eye not only of a gardener but of an architect.

And now perhaps Mr and Mrs Smith will go out into their own gardens and put these principles into practice. On the other hand, they will probably do no such thing. Long experience has taught me that whereas people will take advice about love, and about money, and about nearly all the problems which beset us in life, they will scarcely ever take advice about their gardens. Well . . . it may not really matter much, so long as they love them.

Postscript

The personal preferences of a great gardener must always be of interest to the rest of us, and I hope that Sir Eric will forgive me for quoting half a dozen of his own special loves.

Erythronium revolutum. This is a particularly beautiful variety of the Dog's-tooth Violet, with reflexing cream-tinged purple petals and pale yellow anthers. It rises from a luxurious bed of richly marbled foliage. All the Dog's-tooth Violets are exquisite and should be far more widely grown, but this is the finest.

Trillium grandiflorum. Otherwise known as the White Wood Lily. If I had to choose a flower to personify the 'Spirit of the Woodlands', this is the one I should name . . . pure white, tri-petalled, springing with sheer joy from its soft green leaves. But it must have a wood to grow in, or at least fairly constant shade and a moist peaty soil.

Mertensia virginica. The Virginian Cowslip. This is an old-fashioned flower and a strangely neglected one, maybe because it demands the same sort of conditions as the trillium. It looks like a very beautiful purplish cowslip with a drooping head.

Rhododendron Souliei. Considering the vast number of rhododendron species and hybrids in the domain which he controls,

RHODODENDRON
SOULIEI

ERYTHRONIUM
REVOLUTUM

MERTENSIA
VIRGINICA

TRILLIUM
GRANDIFLORUM

Sir Eric must have had very good reasons for picking this out for our special attention. If you visit the gardens in May to inspect them on the spot you will understand why he did so.

Nurserymen often write such admirable prose that I shall lift the description of *R. Souliei* straight from the catalogue of Mr James Russell, Sunningdale Nurseries, Windlesham:

> Slow-growing, it advances branch by branch like some delicate piece of furniture. The heart-shaped leaves are a shining green, paler beneath. The flowers in flat-topped trusses, varying in colour from pink to white, are supported on very sticky glandular pedicels, and are of perfect shape. The young growth is equally beautiful; scarlet bracts drop to leave young lettuce-green leaves unfolding, which acquire with age a wonderful bluish sheen.

Thank you, Mr Russell.

Primula Vialii. This is a most unusual primula, which might be mistaken by the uninitiated for a wild orchid. It is conical in shape, and when coming into flower displays its first colour by a brilliant scarlet tip. As the days go by it fluffs out at the base in a flurry of pale mauve. It has two great advantages: it will flourish in total shade, and will flower all through July, when most of the other primulas have long since departed. Further details in appendix.

Autumn crocus. One of the richest splendours of the dying year is the *double* autumn crocus, with its petticoats of pale ivory silk that slowly glow to a deep lavender. This, at least, is how I see it, though if you are ordering it you might be wiser to ask for Colchicum hybrid, Water-lily variety. This really is a spectacular new-comer; when you see it glowing in the grass you feel that a film star must just have passed by and de-corsaged herself in a moment of temperamental abandon. Though I agree with Sir Eric that all the autumn crocuses are a delight, the Water-lily Colchicums must really be awarded the Oscar.

They cost five shillings a bulb, at the moment of writing. To avoid disappointment—for they have a habit of disappearing after the first year—plant them in pure sand.

CHAPTER FOUR

ALL FOR THREEPENCE

THERE can be no story-line to this book, nor any pattern to the picture, and were we to try to impose one the result would be as distressing as the photograph of a Persian kitten stuffed into a top-hat. About a hundred of these monstrosities arrive on my desk every year, sent in by professional animal photographers who wish them to be included in a Cat Calendar which I put together during the long winter evenings. The photographs are briskly returned. I do not happen to like Persian kittens being stuffed into top hats, or pushed into pianos or balanced on the tops of typewriters, particularly when they are also obviously being half throttled by large pink bows. Kittens should be allowed to walk where they choose, which is seldom where the photographer wants them.

And so should the authors of gardening books. We will therefore proceed with cat-like tread, pausing here to chase a leaf or climb a tree or simply lie down in the shade.

However, though there can be no story-line we may perhaps establish a sense of continuity. And since in the last chapter we paid a visit to the Savill Gardens, on the principle that it is part of the gardener's essential education to learn what is going on in the world outside his own little plot, let us now prepare to visit another great garden, as though our coats and hats were still hanging in the hall and the car still standing outside the door.

The garden we are going to visit is one of the most famous in the world—the Royal Botanic Gardens at Kew—and this time we shall have a companion by our side. An author tempts providence when he brings on to the stage a character who has already appeared in his previous books; the reader is apt to suspect that his inventive powers are flagging and that he cannot think of anybody new. However, the friend whom I called Marius[1] has been so constant a companion of my gardening life that I could not keep him out, even if I wanted to. Marius, in the past ten years, has changed very little. True, his hair is streaked with grey, and he has put on a little weight, but mentally he is as gay and stimulating as ever.

He has three qualities which delight me.

Firstly, his mystery. Although I have known Marius for twenty years I still have no clear idea of what he is, nor what he does. All I know is that he is a denizen of that shadowy No-Man's-Land which lies somewhere between the Foreign Office and the Secret Service.

[1] He appeared in the 'Merry Hall' trilogy.

Secondly, his erudition. He got a first in Greats at Oxford which he followed up by a comparable distinction in Paris after only two years at the Sorbonne. While still in his twenties he was casually producing, at his own expense and in extremely limited editions, essays on such subjects as Chinese ceramics and Edgar Allen Poe's Theory of the Universe as expressed in the forgotten masterpiece *Eureka*. He related it, in some obscure way, with the Einstein theory, but I doubt whether Poe, or Einstein, or even Marius really understood it.

And Marius's third quality—his kindness, especially to myself. I have a rag-tag-and-bobtail mind, as disorderly as a muddled work-basket. Blunted needles, skeins of bright thread all tangled up, pieces of fabric with designs begun and abandoned. When I am with Marius he makes me forget these shortcomings. He solaces me, and imparts to these lacunae of ignorance an element of virtue.

'You should not distress yourself, my dear Beverley, that you are not a scholar. You are something more important— a story-teller. Nonetheless, I should have thought that in these gardens a modicum of scholarship might have enhanced one's interest. After all, Kew began—as it were— with Julius Caesar.'

We were walking across Queen Elizabeth's lawn one sunny afternoon. He paused and looked across the lazy Thames, shading his eyes from the glitter of the water.

'In fact,' he said, 'it probably began precisely here.'

Whereupon he spoke in Latin. '*Caesar cognito consilio eorum ad flumen Tamesim exercitum duxit; quod flumen uno omnino loco pedibus, atque hoc aegre, transiri potest.*'[1]

[1] 'Having obtained knowledge of their plans, Caesar led his army as far as the River Thames, which can be crossed at one place only on foot, and that with difficulty.'

'Marius, this is going too far.'

'I should not have thought that a simple passage from Caesar's Gallic War was going too far; one usually associates such exercises with the Lower Fourth.'

'What are you talking about?'

'I was recalling the fact that in the year 54 B.C. Caesar led his army to the Thames, and that this particular stretch of the Thames, throughout history, has always been shallower than any other. However, I suppose I must remind you that Caesar did not have too easy a passage. Our rude forebears had prepared a welcome for him in the form of sharp stakes driven into the river-bed and hidden by the water. If you were in a mood for skin-diving you might find yourself impaled on them to this day.'

Marius was right. Incredible as it may seem, those stakes are still holding firm in the river today; two thousand years of time and tide have failed to dislodge them. According to the Thames Conservancy some of the stakes were recently found to be so sharp and strong that they constituted a danger to navigation and had to be removed. If ever we needed a tribute to the sturdiness of British oak, it is here.

We walked on, and came near to the Pagoda which is Kew's most prominent landmark. Marius paused and looked up at it. 'This has always struck me as a crazy eminence,' he said, 'and it has certainly witnessed some crazy happenings. Do you remember? But no . . . you never remember anything. . . . During one of his frenzies the lamentable King George the Third decided that he had a divine mission to climb to the top of the Pagoda, and it took four footmen three quarters of an hour to persuade him that he was mistaken. That would have made a wonderful subject for a cartoon by Rowlandson. George was the classic example of the tragic comedian; he even had an occasional flash of wit. He managed to purloin a copy of *King Lear*, which his physicians had forbidden him to read. And when he had a temporary reversion to sanity, and his elder daughters were first allowed to visit him, he said to them, "I am like poor Lear; but thank God, I have no Regan, no Goneril, but three Cordelias."

'But whatever else we may say about him, at least he loved these gardens.' He smiled. 'Yes, Kew has certainly had its share of eccentrics. You see that building in the distance?' He pointed in the direction of a charming Georgian house, half hidden by a high wall. 'That was once the residence of the first Duke of Cambridge, and I have just been reading about him in the admirable history of Doctor Turrill. Listen to this . . .'

He drew a well-worn volume from under his arm and proceeded to read:

> In his later years the Duke of Cambridge became very deaf. He frequently attended services in St Anne's Church on Kew Green and always sat right in the front of the church where he was seen by the whole congregation. It is said that he made a running commentary on the service in a loud tone of voice. A common occurrence was to hear him say in reply to the clergyman's 'Let us pray' a kindly 'By all means' or in answer to a prayer for rain, 'Amen, but you won't get it till the wind changes.' When the commandment 'Thou shalt do no murder' was read, the clearly heard voice of the Duke stated, 'I don't; I leave that to my brother Ernest.'[1]

[1] From *The Royal Botanic Gardens, Kew* by W. B. Turrill, O.B.E., D.SC. (London: Herbert Jenkins, 1959). By kind permission of the publishers.

For a moment he was silent. Then, as though speaking to himself, he murmured, 'Thou shalt do no murder.' He closed the volume and stared across the lawn at the little Georgian house—Cambridge Cottage as it is now called.

'And that reminds me that I have a story to tell you about that little building—a story of my own. Perhaps you might use it, one of these days, in one of your novels of detection. You see . . . it is the story of a murder.'

I hardly dare to imagine how Sir George Taylor, the eminent director of the greatest botanical gardens in the world, will react when he reads what I have just written. In spite of its radiant vistas of daffodils, its choruses of dancing cherries, its noble trees, its hosts of roses and its dreaming waters—in spite of the perpetual panorama that draws the crowds—Kew is, first and foremost, a scientific institution. It plays an important part in the economy of the Commonwealth. Because of Kew, and because of the tireless and usually anonymous researches of its workers, vast areas of distant territories have blossomed and borne fruit, and many new techniques have been perfected in the eternal war which man is obliged to wage against the enemies of natural fertility—the pests, the parasites, and all the other malevolent forces of destruction. Kew's relationship to Nature might be compared with that of a diagnostician, or a surgeon, or even a sort of super family solicitor . . . guarding the family documents, guiding the family policy, and studying every opportunity of wise investment for future development.

However, I am not writing for economists but for the average man, impelled by a very genuine desire to persuade him to pass through Kew's magic turnstiles. For I believe that in the heart of every man there sleeps a gardener, and that Kew will help him to discover what sort of gardener he is destined to be . . . as we shall see, from the following story.

'Mine is a murder story,' said Marius. 'And it was set in this very garden, on just such an evening as this.'

We walked across to the Cottage, and seated ourselves on one of the benches in a quiet corner.

'Yes,' he continued, 'it was just as it is now, except that today the cherries are taller and the magnolias have climbed higher up the wall. The essential part of the garden—the garden of medicinal herbs, which is all around us—was already very much in existence. However, I am anticipating.

'I was still a schoolboy, with no very strong convictions as to the sort of career I wished to follow. I had many passing enthusiasms, and at that time I was toying with the idea of becoming a physician. And I had always believed, since I emerged from my perambulator, that when one is studying any particular science one should begin at the beginning. So I decided that a medical career should begin with the study of herbs and the various therapies that have been evolved from them. It might be profitable, I thought, when I had reached the eminence of Harley Street (which I had every intention of doing) and when I was prescribing for some dyspeptic duchess a pill with a base of rhubarb, to be able to divert her with some anecdotes about the campaigns of Charles the Fifth, who—as I need hardly remind you— was first responsible for bringing rhubarb to Europe. It is one of the ironies of history that in spite of his vast expenditure of blood and treasure his sole enduring monument is a stick of rhubarb. However, that is by the way.

'As I was saying, it was on just such an evening as this,

clear and sunny, with a faint breeze from the south. I was sitting on this very bench, studying some notes I had made about amaranthus. I was particularly interested in this herb because my reading of Culpeper had instructed me that it was—I think I quote correctly—"an excellent qualifier of the unruly actions and passions of Venus"—and as a school-boy of fourteen I was already beginning to be faintly troubled by the attentions of this goddess, in the shape of the headmaster's daughter. I decided that a few leaves of amaranthus, discreetly nibbled during evening prep, might help me to pursue my studies with less distraction. And then . . . I looked up, and I saw her.'

'The headmaster's daughter?'

Marius frowned. 'Certainly not. The murderess. At least, she *looked* like a murderess. She was a woman of about fifty, tall and very thin, with a profile not unlike that of the Duke of Wellington. She was dressed in a black cloak and she was standing over there, by that wall.' He waved in the direction with his cane. 'In a moment we will go and see what she was looking at, if it is still there. Meanwhile, I continued to stare at her. She was bent low over one of the plants and she seemed to be caressing it with her hands, as though she had some special affection for it. I remember thinking that if a keeper came along she would earn a reproof, because one is not supposed to touch the plants. Then she straightened herself and turned in my direction, and I could see that she was smiling. It was not a pleasant smile. She walked a few paces down the border, and then again she bent down, with her cloak blowing about her, and began to caress another plant. There really is no other word for the gestures she was making. I was able to mark her exact position because she was next to a group of wild lettuces . . .'

Suddenly he broke off and turned to me with a frown.

'Do *you* believe the legend about Pythagoras and the lettuces?'

'I'm afraid I've never even heard of it.'

'No? I wonder how it could have escaped you. He was supposed to have lived on them almost exclusively. Which, to say the least of it, I find surprising. The only geometricians one has known have had enormous appetites. You must remind me to speak to you more about lettuces one of these days, not that I know so much about them. I doubt if I can even pronounce their Chinese name correctly. The nearest I can get to it is "Chin-chin". One's Chinese is not what it was.'

'Marius, you disappoint me.'

'And I shall bore you, no doubt, if I do not get on with my little story. Well, there is not much more to it. The witch departed, walking into the sunset with that terrible smile. And I crept over to the border to see the two plants which she had been caressing. The first was . . . hemlock. And even *you*, with your perpetual pretence of ignorance, do not have to be reminded that this was the poison which snuffed out the life of one of the greatest men whose intelligence ever lit the world—Socrates. And the second plant was . . . belladonna. The Deadly Nightshade.' He glanced up to the sky, which had grown overcast. 'An apposite name, for the light is fading. We had best hurry, if we are to see them clearly.'

We walked over the soft lawn on which the evening dew was already gathering. And there they were, in the precise spot that he had indicated, marked by a warning sign, THESE BERRIES ARE POISONOUS. You would not have thought so, to look at them.

The hemlock—*Conium maculatum*—was as dainty as a

cluster of Queen Anne's lace, growing by a stream in the meadow. The belladonna *Atropa belladonna*, with its discreet flower of smoky blue, would have been lost in the most modest herbaceous border. But as Marius had reminded me, the root of the one had put an end to Socrates, and three berries of the other can kill a child.

'But Marius, you have not told me the end of the story.'

'Oh that?' He smiled. 'I had almost forgotten. A year later, I saw her again. Not in the flesh, but in a photograph. On the front page of the *News of the World*, which I was in the habit of perusing when the classics began to pall. She had been arrested for the murder of her husband who had died in mysterious circumstances after a brief and agonizing illness. The whole basis of the prosecution rested on a tin of weed killer, and on the question of whether it had, or had not, been opened. The defence proved conclusively that it had *not*.'

He leant forward, as though he were going to pluck a leaf of the belladonna. Then he drew back again.

'You see, she had no need to open it. When the reporters interviewed her, after she had been acquitted, they were at pains to vindicate her character. She had always been devoted, they said, to her dog. And she had been equally devoted to her little garden.'

I trust that this story may not put ideas into anybody's head, and that the turnstiles of Kew may not thereby be darkened by the shadows of potential Crippens. I told it merely to illustrate the fact that at Kew there is something to satisfy every temperament and every mood.

Those who have a fancy for the macabre—and the vast

sale of detective stories suggests that most of us have our morbid moments—might think it worth while, after a trip to the Herb Garden, to pay a visit to the nearby museum, where they will find more about these poisons, and many other examples of Nature at her most murderous. They will see, for example, a very pretty picture of the aconitum, with its blue flowers that brighten so many old-fashioned borders. By its side they will note a strange contrivance made from rushes, which in certain countries is used as a form of muzzle to prevent sheep from eating the plant, for the roots contain the most virulent poison. They will be reminded—as Miss Daphne du Maurier also reminded us in *My Cousin Rachel*— that tens of thousands of suburban gardens annually produce enough deadly poisons to equip a whole generation of Borgias, in the shape of the golden-tasselled laburnums whose seeds contain the toxic principle *cytisine*. Even a handful of these seeds will kill a horse.

And they may be surprised—as I have often been—to discover that so many of the deadliest flowers and plants have been dressed by Nature in the prettiest and most innocent guises. The flowers of the dire hemlock are so virginal that they might deck an altar, and though the little autumn crocus is as exquisite as a fairy it is poisonous in flower and leaf and root. Perhaps the most deceptively demure blossom in the world—you will find it in one of the hothouses—is the flower of the Cocaine Bush. It looks as harmless as a daisy, and it is difficult to realize that it has been the cause of sending many men and women to a living hell.

Here, in short, is Kew's Chamber of Horrors. Here, by the side of these evil innocents, we can see the ways in which men have perverted them—the poisoned arrows that still hiss through the jungles of British Guiana, the blowpipes whose sinister missiles are tipped with the swiftest killer of all, the poison of the Ipoh Plant. And ranged around them are the cruelties which Nature has inflicted on her own creations—the freaks and monstrosities of the vegetable kingdom, that recall the horrors of an old-fashioned circus: pineapples with three heads, cancerous tomatoes, pears linked together like Siamese twins . . .

Perhaps it is time that we left these things, and took a turn in the fresh air.

CHAPTER FIVE

BELIEVE IT OR NOT

S O FAR in this survey, I have refrained from discussing the *obvious* reasons for visiting Kew. I have not paused at any of the trees, nor lingered in the water gardens, nor even taken a stroll through the Rhododendron Dell. This method of approach has been deliberate. The casual visitor will probably discover these things of his own accord. At every season of the year the notice board by the main entrance will tell him of any special delights which are to be inspected on the day of his visit. And the botanist, or the would-be botanist, is surely capable of reading the labels on any particular plant and, if he needs further information, pursuing his studies in the libraries or the museums.

76

I am casting my net for a wider public, for those many people—and they are a very large number indeed—to whom the idea of a visit to Kew makes no appeal whatsoever. Here we might again cite the technique of Macaulay. In his determination to bring the fashionable young people of his day to the study of their country's history he employed every trick of the literary trade; it is hardly an exaggeration to say that he would brighten a dull point of constitutional law with the sudden gleam of a dandy's waistcoat.

On this same principle I want to flash the spotlight on to Kew's great Australian House, which is one of the most fascinating of its several conservatories. Not only because of the butterfly brilliance of the flowers that we shall meet inside it, but because of the extraordinary sense it gives us of stepping out of Europe into a totally different climate and environment. A walk through this miniature Crystal Palace will give the average man a truer impression of the 'atmosphere' of the continent than any amount of travel books or television 'shorts'; indeed, any young people who think of emigrating to Australia would be well advised to take themselves to Kew for the sole purpose of visiting this house—to see what it would 'do' to them. That it would 'do' something is quite certain; the reaction is immediate and overwhelming. As soon as we push open the glass door we enter a new botanical world and—since botany is a sort of lowest common denominator of all the sciences—we have a sense of entering a world that is also 'new' in a great many other ways, biologically, even spiritually. It is almost like walking down a Devonshire lane and suddenly encountering a duck-billed platypus blinking amiably from the hedgerow. These salutary shocks, as I suggested, begin at the moment of entry, for facing the door is a magnificent specimen of one of the

77

world's strangest shrubs, the Bottlebrush (*Callistemon speciosus*). It is a flamboyant, extravagant and altogether unlikely creation; the arrogant scarlet flowers are like fantasies of spun glass tied to the branches by a modern decorator. Once, paying my annual visit to this phenomenon in June, I found myself standing next to two young ladies from Paris. For some time they regarded it in silence. Then one of them turned to the other and said, '*C'est magnifique, mais ce n'est pas une fleur.*' Which seemed to sum up the situation very well.

Incidentally, the Bottlebrush will grow happily in a cold greenhouse, and in sheltered valleys of Devonshire and Cornwall it flourishes out of doors.

Within the confines of a glass house, the Australian scene can be reproduced only in miniature; but no sensitive person, walking through the strangely tinted shadows of that Continent's flora, can fail to receive the impression of being transported to a world that is different from anything he has ever known before, a world in which the scents and the shapes and the colours speak in a totally unfamiliar language. And —paradoxically—a very old world, too. This impression of 'pre-history' is to be explained perhaps by the fact that for millions of years vast tracts of the Continent have enjoyed conditions of shelter and isolation—from the ravages not only of man but of animals and birds, and wind and weather —which have been known in no other part of the world. 'The Flora of Western Australia has no known beginning yet it is believed to have been of *Antarctic* origin,' writes the Curator of the State Herbarium at Perth. He points to the map to show us the causes of this uniqueness. Guarded by the Ocean from the north and the west and the south, guarded from the east by a million square miles of almost impassable desert, the flowers have blossomed and seeded and been reborn in an almost infinite cycle. These are the flowers whom Gray might have been describing when he wrote his all too famous couplet

> Full many a flower is born to blush unseen,
> And waste its sweetness on the desert air.

As we suggested before, 'men come to gardens by many roads and learn to be gardeners by many chances'. But the garden path is a two-way traffic, and may lead a man to horizons which he never dreamed of. Let us give flesh and substance to this generalization.

Mr and Mrs Smith, of South Hackney, take their son Robert, on a summer afternoon, to Kew Gardens. Total expenditure—exclusive of bus fares—ninepence. Robert is a problem child and has reached the age of thirteen without showing any inclination to adapt himself to the life which lies ahead. Listlessly he follows his parents round the gardens, kicking at the turf, yawning at the roses, resenting the fact that he is not permitted to turn on his transistor radio.

By chance, Mr Smith decides that he would like to take a look at the Economic House. They push open the doors and walk inside. Suddenly, young Robert is confronted by a banana. Not a *real* banana—for real bananas, as Robert is only too well aware, only come on barrows. But this particular banana, which greets his amazed attention, is a different cup of tea. It has actually attached itself, by some mystic process, to a living plant; it is surrounded by strange, lusty, glossy leaves, that are also obviously alive; and there it is, sticking out as bold as brass, pretending to be a banana. Something happens in Robert's mind, something which seems to turn his whole crazy 'civilized' world upside down. The banana comes to life. It detaches itself from the barrow, where it has hitherto belonged, and it attaches itself to Nature. Robert has an extraordinary sense that the curtain is rising on a scene in a pantomime, in which the stage is overhung by giant branches laden with strange flowers and monstrous fruits—a scene glittering with mysterious lights that never shone on land or sea.

You can guess the end of the story, of course. Young Robert leaves Kew with a gleam of excitement in his eyes. Very soon he has joined the merchant navy. When his ship berths at Singapore, he goes absent, strikes out into the jungle, catches an obscure fever, and is rescued in a state of near coma by the beautiful little daughter of a rich banana merchant. Inevitably, he recovers, is adopted into the family circle, and begins to grow bananas. Very soon, Robert is growing bigger, better and brighter bananas than have ever been grown before; by the time he has reached the age of twenty he is head of the firm, has married the daughter of the firm, and is on the way to becoming a millionaire. And though his parents, Mr and Mrs Smith of South Hackney, are very proud of his success, they are beginning to grow a little weary of bananas, of which an immense crate is delivered to them on the first of every month. The banana is a fruit that tends to pall.

Such was the story of young Robert, and such might be the story, with countless variations, of thousands of young people who pass through those magic turnstiles.

But will the crowds sense those stories? Will they be able to trace them in the veins of the leaves and hear them in the whispers of the branches? When one's job is to tell stories, every picture tells a story, and one is perpetually astonished that other people do not seem to be able to read them. Watching the crowds at Kew I have noticed, a little sadly, that they so often 'go' for such obvious things—the drifts of daffodils, and the flowering cherries, and the rhododendron walks. They 'go' for the fabulous firework displays of the orchids in the hot-houses, and they will always follow with rapture the antics of a brood of freshly hatched ducklings on the Great Pond. They even 'go' for the serried beds of roses geometrically disposed outside the Palm House—beds from which I, personally, prefer to avert my eyes. They remind me of giant slabs of nougat. I don't like that sort of gardening at all.

However, perhaps I am maligning the crowd. Not all of them always join the big battalions. One of the most heartening prospects of Kew, when one's faith in human nature is at a low ebb, is afforded by the rock gardens. For here, on every day of the year, in every sort of weather, one is quite certain to encounter small groups of devoted gardeners bending low over the beds, studying flowers that are scarcely bigger than a pin's head, and carefully copying down the names from the labels on to scraps of paper which may well be sodden with the rain. To these amiable persons I have given the name of 'Shrinkers', and the fact that they are still in fairly generous supply is one of the few sure proofs that the world has not yet gone to total damnation.

The Nichols theory of 'Shrinking', and its importance in meeting the problems of the twentieth century, has already been advocated in previous volumes so I will not waste too much space on explaining its techniques. Briefly it is based on the belief that everything in the world is getting too big—

flowers, buildings, cities, bombs, in fact almost everything you care to mention—and that the only way back to sanity is to follow the signpost marked 'To Lilliput'.

There is no such signpost at Kew, but there are clearly marked directions to the rock gardens, and it is here that the would-be Lilliputian should wend his way. As he does so he must try to bear in mind the essentials of the Nichols technique, which must always be employed during the contemplation, or indeed the creation, of rock gardens. He must persuade himself that he is growing smaller and smaller and that the rocks are getting larger and larger. He no longer weighs fourteen stone, he no longer treads heavily; he is a tiny floating creature looking up in astonishment at immense torrents of blossom that threaten to engulf him. If he is new to the game it is more than possible that his first essays may bring him into sharp collision with ladies pushing perambulators. If he plays it with too much abandon he may arouse the suspicions of the keepers, who may misconstrue his postures. But if he persists, his spirit will be refreshed, he will learn a great deal about botany without realizing that he is learning anything at all—the only lasting method of education—and, most important of all, when he unbends and straightens himself, and blinks, and becomes again aware of the world around him, he will see it as the foolish and unimportant place it is, compared with the beauties and eternal truths of Lilliput.

Now and again I have wandered through these gardens with Marius, and always I have emerged just a little bit wiser. (And more than just a little bit poorer, too—my pockets stuffed with the backs of envelopes on which are inscribed the names of tiny plants whose cost seems to be in inverse proportion to their size.) To the cultured reader these small scraps of knowledge will seem very *vieux jeu*, but I have never been ashamed to admit my ignorance.

I can still hear Marius's voice, and link it with the flowers of which he was speaking. Thus, when we were suddenly enraptured, in April, by a miniature troop of *Iris reticulata* . . .

'You have doubtless forgotten, my dear Beverley, that the Greeks had a word for it.'

'When I talk to you, Marius, I begin to think that the Greeks had a word for everything.'

'They had. They had a word for the rainbow. And the word was Iris.'

There they were, like a cluster of tiny rainbows, shining against the rocks. Why has nobody ever called the iris the 'rainbow flower'?

Again, when we were studying a cluster of the silver-leaved centaurea, Marius said:

'I should not be surprised, my dear Beverley, if you were to tell me that these exquisite leaves conveyed no suggestion of the human foot?'

He was quite right. They conveyed no such suggestion; they were very much daintier and more decorative. But Marius was correcting himself.

'I beg your pardon. Not the human foot. The foot of the centaur. The centaur in question was a young gentleman called Chiron, who seems to have been quite a prominent personality in Centaur society. He was healed of a wound in the foot by these very leaves. Hence the word 'centaurea'. When you are planting out your next box of *Centaurea gymnocarpa* you may care to remember this fact. And since you have a very vivid imagination, which perhaps compensates for your appalling ignorance, you may hear the thunder of centaurs' hooves.'

'Thank you, Marius. I have a very vivid imagination. And I am appallingly ignorant. But I do hear the echo of those hooves.'

The vast area of our canvas, quite obviously, is leading us astray. Unless we are to linger in the gardens for ever, we must find some way of bringing the story of Kew to a conclusion. Perhaps we might find this by borrowing the technique of the celebrated Mr Ripley, whose 'Believe It or Not' cartoons have given us the title for this chapter.

If Mr Ripley were ever to visit Kew, here are some of the phenomena that might perhaps appeal to him.

BELIEVE IT OR NOT. (KEW VERSION)

1. *A single pod of the orchid* Cynorchis chlorochilon *has been known to contain as many as 3,770,000 seeds.* Three million, seven hundred and seventy thousand. You may wonder who counted them, and how, and in what particular mental home he or she is presently situated; so do I. Anyway, it must be true, because it's 'in the book'.

2. *Apples are roses.* The fact that I was unaware of this elemental fact shows that I know about as much botany as the lady who comes and 'does' on Mondays, Wednesdays and Fridays. But did *you* know that apples were roses? Listen to the supreme authority, Dr Turrill: 'Special mention must be made of the Rose Family (*Rosaceae*) in connection with fruits of its woody members. Not only do many of the plants supplying fruits for human consumption belong to this family—apples, pears, plums, cherries, quinces, apricots, peaches, nectarines, raspberries, blackberries, strawberries —but a very large number of ornamental species such as flowering crabs, mountain ashes and hawthorns.'

84

After which, it is almost obligatory to quote Miss Gertrude Stein. 'A rose is a rose is a rose,' said she. And now, at an advanced stage in life, we learn that a rose is also a raspberry.

3. *The largest flower in the world, to be seen at Kew, has a diameter of 3 feet, weighs 12 to 15 lbs, and is able to hold as much as 12 pints of water.* This, of course, is pure Ripley. One can almost see him drawing it, and setting it next to a profile of a Charleston centenarian who lived for forty years on an exclusive diet of safety-pins. But—believe it or not—this astonishing flower does exist, and you can see a life-size model of it on the first floor of the General Museum, which lies directly behind the Great Pond.

Of all the monstrous fantasies of Nature this blossom— *Rafflesia Arnoldii*—will probably strike the average man as the most evil. It glowers in its case like a giant starfish, with corpse-coloured petals that suggest hungry tongues. It has no stalk, no stem, no leaves; and it is completely parasitic, sucking the life blood from the roots of vines in the darkest forests of Sumatra. The centre gapes open, disclosing a circle of sharp, yellow teeth. It is the sort of flower that one might expect to find glimmering at the entrance to a cave in some poisoned valley of the moon. I strongly recommend it to the attention of all authors of space fiction.

4. *The most mysterious tree in Nature is probably the Maidenhair Tree; it has never been found growing wild in any part of the world.* Of this, as it happens, I was already aware. The Maidenhair Tree (*Ginkgo biloba*) has always held a peculiar fascination for me because of the mystery of its origin. It has been found by the side of ruined temples in China and Japan; and sometimes, in districts such as the remote foothills of Szechuan, botanists have encountered specimens which seemed to have come 'of their own accord'. But always, in the end, research

revealed evidence that man had been there before, even if he had only left behind him a few fragments of pottery or the shell of a buried tomb.

This strange phenomenon is made all the more absorbing because of the tree's immense botanical age. It has been traced back, in the form of fossils, to the early Mesozoic Age, and very close relations to it have been recorded from the Devonian periods—many thousands of years before the British coal mines, in the form of still-living timber, were crashing to the earth, to the wild music of the warm prehistoric rains.

Maybe I have some sort of psychic rapport with this extraordinary tree; before I even knew its name it 'did' something to me. The first specimen I ever saw was in the garden at Broadlands in Hampshire. I reached up for a branch to study it in closer detail, and found myself staring at the leaves in a sort of puzzlement. What did they remind me of? Then I got it. They were the footprints of a prehistoric animal, frozen through the ages in some remote stratum of time. Study them for yourself, and you will see what I mean.

After all this, the beginner may gain the impression that the ginkgo is an expensive exotic, that can only be grown by prehistoric duchesses living in ruined castles in the Southern counties. Not at all. The ginkgo is as tough as they come, and as tolerant . . . tolerant of temperature, tolerant of soil, tolerant even of the city smog. When I was last staying in New York, in 72nd St, at the corner of Park Avenue, and when I set out for my daily promenade in Central Park, my path took me past a line of ginkgos. They were set in a tiny patch of soil in a concrete frame, they were subjected to the perpetual assaults of a corrupted atmosphere, and they were obliged to withstand extremes of cold and of heat. Yet there they were, flourishing like green bay trees, with the mink-clad armies of Park Avenue matrons tugging their poodles past their indestructible trunks. I longed to pluck the sleeve of one of these matrons and say to her, 'Do you realize that you are walking past fifty million years of natural history? Do you realize that if you allowed your poodle to pause at one of those trunks, as he obviously wishes to do, he would be, as it were, sending a personal message, through time and space, to a pterodactyl?'

You will find a magnificent specimen at Kew, which was planted just over two centuries ago. It still flowers profusely every May, but its crowning hours come in October, when the leaves turn pale gold overnight with the first of the frosts, as though King Midas had let his fingers stray across them. Should you decide to invest in one you will find a few practical details in the appendix.

'And now'—as commentators croon in the travelogues—'we bid farewell to Kew', because we have many other places to talk about. The reader of the last three chapters may well complain that they have been something of a hotch-potch. I am aware of this. However—like Mr Ripley and the afore-said travelogue commentators—my main purpose in this long story has been to impart information painlessly, to convey to the reader my own sense of excitement, and to persuade him to visit Kew at the beginning rather than the end of his career. For only too often in this life one's really vital discoveries are made some twenty years too late.

CHAPTER SIX

THE GLORY OF GREY

A s WE were saying before we turned the page, one's really vital discoveries are made, only too often, some twenty years too late. The island of one's dreams looms on the horizon; one sails into harbour and steps ashore—only to discover that there are footsteps on the sand and empty tins among the rocks. Somebody has got there before. As it is with places so it is with people. If only one had known him, or her, twenty years ago—how different life might have been! But one didn't. Somebody got there before.

Which is a gloomy beginning to a chapter celebrating one of the happiest passages in my gardening life.

This theory about discovering everything too late applies with particular force to the gardener. The most obvious example is afforded by ignorance of the nature of the soil. A young couple—or even more distressfully, a middle-aged couple—find an ideal cottage in apparently perfect surroundings, scrape up enough money to buy it, and start off on the most exciting adventure that life is likely to offer them, this side of the grave—the making of a garden. Before they have been at it for a fortnight they learn that nine-tenths of the things they want to grow will never be worth the planting, because the soil is full of chalk. Why didn't they know? Why had nobody warned them? Well . . . I have been warning them for years, in no uncertain terms, but nobody seems to have taken much notice. I suppose that this is one of the things which one has to find out for oneself.

So it is with grey. It has taken me over thirty years of tireless experiment to discover the glory of grey in the garden, to reach the stage where I can write that it now seems to me as important as any of the colours on the gardener's palette, and maybe even more important. However, as this is one of those statements which is calculated to produce cries of 'Question!', and even faint hisses from the gallery, I should mention that the colour 'grey' is here intended to include all the variations cited in our old friend *Roget's Thesaurus*, which mentions 'silver, steel, slate, ivory, pearl, frost, cream and alabaster'. To which we might perhaps add our own contributions of 'oyster-shell, magnolia, jade-grey and Atlantic foam', with the accent on the 'foam'.

For all these colours, at the moment of writing, are breaking in a great wave of leafy spray in the bed outside the window of my music room. And the moment of writing is November the fourth.

There should be no day in the year when the serious gardener has nothing to show for his pains, but it will be generally agreed that the first Sunday in November is not normally regarded as a day when, after church, one can linger in the porch, dropping mysterious hints that something very splendid is happening in one's garden, something that is almost certainly happening in nobody else's. And that, please, would they come and look at it?

They came only a few hours ago. The vicar, and the organist and the nice young man who hands round the prayer books, and a faintly bewildered couple from Canada who had not been to church at all, but had been dragged out of the graveyard, where they had been paying a pilgrimage to Vancouver's tomb. All these respectable persons—at least, the Canadian couple *looked* respectable, and shrank back in horror when offered a small glass of dry sherry—will testify to the fact that on the morning of November 4, 1966, Mr Beverley Nichols transported them to his garden and proved to them that something very splendid was indeed happening, in the shape of that great Atlantic breaker of leaf and flower, stippled with foam and streaked with silver.

The vicar, who did not refuse the glass of sherry, said the ultimate word. He turned back at the garden gate, for a last look at the border, which was glinting and shimmering in the wind.

'It makes one feel like rewriting the Benedicite,' he said. 'All ye grey things of the Earth, bless ye the Lord.'

Until you have got grey into your head, in all its exquisite gradations, you are like an artist trying to paint a portrait with one hand tied behind his back. At all times of the year it is a source of radiance and delight. In the winter it lights up the woodland with the trunks of the silver birches, the bluish steel of the silver cypresses, and the strange, spectral stems of the *Rubus Cockburnianus*, which look as though they had been dipped in phosphorescent paint. There is plenty of grey, too, in the winter garden, even if we were to confine ourselves to the rosemaries, the lavenders, and the sages. In the spring the palette swiftly broadens, with the frosted leaves of the silver pears and the silver poplars (though, when we study them closely, we see that they would need to be reproduced in platinum) and the luminous underleaves of the silver buddleia (*Buddleia Fallowiana*), which forms so charming a complement to a clump of that old-fashioned favourite, Lamb's Ear (*Stachys lanata*).

However, it is not till late summer and autumn that grey really comes into its own. But I can only make this vivid to the reader by reverting to the technique of the diarist, who must begin every section of his memoirs with a date. A page or two ago we mentioned such a date—the first Sunday in November—and for a moment a few figures made their appearance, the vicar, the organist, the nice young man who hands round the prayer books, and the peculiar couple from Vancouver who, now I come to think of it, might play a quite sinister role in one of the many detective stories that I shall never live to write. These persons have now departed. Luncheon has been served and, one hopes, digested. The diary opens . . .

Today is November the fourth and I am writing this in a rather peculiar position, twisted into the porch of the music room, so that I can have a comprehensive view of everything that is going on outside.

A great deal *is* going on. Anthony and Trollop[1] have dis-covered a hedgehog emerging from the heather bed, and are sitting on each side of it, at a safe distance. They look like two Egyptian statues, carved from ebony, confronted by some strange form of sacrifice which they have never en-countered before. If there must be feline blood-sports in the garden these are the sorts that I prefer, because nobody is likely to get hurt; indeed, even as I watch, the hedgehog retreats into the heather bed, and Anthony and Trollop, bored with the whole proceedings, stalk off to inspect the goldfish in the lily-pond, where their sport is likely to be even less rewarding. Then the garden door opens and the man from Young's comes in to take away the garden chairs which are to be recovered for next summer; opens again to admit two small boys who have called for the windfalls from the pear tree; opens yet again for an obviously insane woman who pokes her head round the corner, catches sight of me sitting in the porch, registers extreme terror and disappears. Country life is full of these pleasing diversions.

But it is the horticultural goings on that concern us, and these are centred at the other end of the garden, where Page is engaged in carting away to the compost heap a small mountain of debris which has accumulated over the week-end during a very energetic bout of clearing up. If we study the ingredients of the mountain we shall realize how much glory has departed from the garden with the frosts of the past few days. All the dahlias, which lie at the bottom of the heap in a soggy unappetizing mass. All the zinnias, which were spectacular only a week ago—a blazing carnival of

---

[1] My feline companions at the time when these words were written, now—for reasons too complicated to be detailed—residing in a stately home in the County of Wiltshire.

colour which degenerated, overnight, into a sad shambles of massacred petals. All the asters and all the border chrysanthemums. Most of the tobacco flowers, though a few clumps of the pure whites, sheltered by the branches of the copper beech, are still immaculate. All the nemesias, the verbenas and the heliotropes. All gone.

This does not mean that the garden is totally devoid of colour. Indeed, compared with most people's gardens, there is quite a lot. Even from my cramped position in the porch my eye is caught by a drift of the lilac-coloured *Physostegia virginiana*, quite unfrosted. This is surely one of the most neglected of all the autumn glories; a cluster of it looks like an inspired sweep of Monet's brush, heavily laden with a pigment that I have called 'lilac' because lilac is a colour of many moods and intonations. And there is another drift of 'lilac' in the veronicas, over there in the far corner . . . some of them, even at this unpropitious hour, still trembling into bud, like innocent children, thinly clad, opening a door on to a frosty world whose perils they have not yet apprehended. Yes, there is still a great deal to see, a great deal by which we may be enchanted . . . strings of coral costume jewellery on the *Berberis Wilsonae*, more Monet passages in the *Daboecia cantabrica* (which might come more vividly to your mind if I simply called it the Irish bog heather) . . . echoes of spring and buttercup meadows in the last late blossoms of *Potentilla fruticosa arbuscula*. Last, but by no means least, a brave challenge of fuchsias underneath the pear tree. Since we seem to be in a mood when similes are cheap and plentiful, I would compare these with ballet dancers, huddled together in a little group backstage in Covent Garden, at the end of the performance, drawing around them their cloaks of pink and rose.

But all these flowers are *survivors*, stragglers on a field of battle which has been largely decimated by the onslaughts of the weather, bravely clinging to their coloured flags before the winds and the rains batter them to the ground. Only in the shining regiments of the greys are the ranks still unbroken.

And now, because the sun has come out again, we can leave our cramped vantage point in the porch, step outside, and look more closely.

The grey and silver border, which is about thirty feet by five feet, runs the full length of the west wall of the cottage, overflows on to the grey stones of the little terrace, and clambers up the old brick walls. In order that this exposition may not degenerate into a mere clutter of words Willie McClaren has drawn an impressionistic picture of it as it was when he first saw it in mid-October. No drawing in black and white could give more than the faintest impression of its beauty, particularly as some of the leaves and flowers are so small that one needs a microscope to appreciate them; and sometimes one has to wait for the wind to make the leaves dance and reveal their silver undercoats. But at least the drawing should help to focus your mind on what part of the border we are looking at.

Let us begin with the background, as though we were designing a stage set. What can we do about climbers? Well, silver climbers are few and far between, but there are one or two of such delicate beauty that we cannot afford to neglect them, and of all these I would put first the silver ivy, which Willie has marked A in our drawing:

Hedera Helix Glacier. The word 'Glacier' for this ivy is well chosen; it really does look as if the winter's frosts were still lingering on the grey-green leaves. Unlike many other ornamental ivies, which always seem to look rather 'common'—if one is still permitted to use that word—there is nothing yellow or striped or mottled about this beautiful creature. Most of the 'ornamental' ivies remind one of middle-aged women who spend a small fortune on keeping their hair gold; the lady Glacier suggests a young woman who has spent a very large fortune because she prefers herself in silver.

In spite of all this rather *Vogue* atmosphere, the lady Glacier is as tough as they come and a quick grower that can be guaranteed to put on about four feet in a year.

The second silver climber is called:

Helichrysum microphyllum (B in our drawing). This has chalk-white stems and leaves of the palest sage, and since it has a fairly open habit both the stalks and the leaves are seen to their fullest advantage. Unlike the ivy this is not a hardy perennial, and must be planted afresh every spring. But it takes very easily from cuttings and towards the end of the summer should be producing a glittering fountain of foliage reaching a height of about five feet.

These are the only two climbers in our colour range with which I have experimented to date, but there are several others which will be included next year if there is room for them.

Before we leave the climbers I must draw your attention to one exception in our colour range, marked C in the picture:

Clematis florida Sieboldii. This—pale cream with a wine-coloured rosette in the centre— is one of the most precious in the whole miraculous family of clematis. As we are concentrating on greys and silvers it has no real place in the border, because of those coloured rosettes in the centre, but I like to think of them as cups of wine held aloft over the silvery host.

Now for the main body of the border. The three most brilliantly shining clumps of all, each marked D, are provided by:

Senecio Cineraria Ramparts. This must be the mainstay of any grey group; even on the dullest days the leaves have a luminous sheen. In full sunshine they sparkle like newly minted metal and by moonlight they glow like the wings of a moth. Moreover, these leaves are carved in a design more delicate and rhythmical than any acanthus. Although the plants in our picture were not bedded out till the end of April they are now sturdy bushes three feet tall. And although they have been constantly cut and taken indoors to make special bunches they have spread so thickly that not an inch of earth is to be seen beneath them.

If you stand and stare at these fabulous creatures for a minute or so and then turn sharply round to scan the rest of the garden, the whole picture seems, by comparison, drab and lifeless. It isn't, of course. The grass is still green, the autumn leaves still burn brightly, there is still a lilt of purple in the heathers. But your eye has been put out by the special radiance of the silver and it takes you several minutes to get back to normal.

Now for height. The crest of the wave, marked E, is provided by:

Artemisia arborescens. This is the tallest of the artemisias, and as you will observe from the picture, has reached a height of over four feet. It gives the effect of a giant silver fern, and although it is apparently so frail and feathery it never flops about, and even after a heavy shower it soon shakes the drops from its silver hair.

The centre of the wave, as we have seen, is provided by the *Senecio Cineraria*, but perhaps the most important part of all is the foreground, because this really does give the effect of foam sweeping up a beach, the forward thrust of water that surges in front of the breakers on a windy day. This effect is produced by three plants that are quite essential, two of which appear in our illustration.

Helichrysum petiolatum (marked F). One of the most remarkable characteristics of this plant is the rapidity of its growth. The four plants in my border were originally a dozen; the other eight had to be scrapped because they soon had no elbow room. Indeed, if we were in need of extra climbers this helichrysum would serve the purpose.

Artemisia Stelleriana (marked G). This has especially delicate foliage, like a silver daisy, to which family, indeed, it is related. Of all the greys and silvers we have mentioned so far, this is the only one to tarnish with the frost—though 'tarnish' is perhaps a misleading word for the pale sheen of gold that comes over the leaves.

Helichrysum leucophytum. One of the tallest, probably the toughest, and certainly the easiest to strike from cuttings.

Now for the flowers, as opposed to the leaves. My own feeling, when designing a border such as this, is that the fewer the flowers, the better. Even white flowers seem to mar the perfection of the picture, and though a clump of madonna lilies may look exquisite—for a few days—the green of their leaves is too outspoken. There is a great temptation to introduce a few delicate pinks and blues through the medium of, say, clumps of dianthus and pale blue flax, but I think that it is better resisted. Imagine a very beautiful woman with white hair in a dress of pale grey satin. She doesn't clutter herself up with a lot of coloured jewellery; she sticks to pearls.

So it is in our border. We stick to pearls, and here are two of them, using the word 'pearl' as a floral symbol. The first, marked H, is . . .

Anaphalis triplinervis. This is a semi-everlasting flower of the daisy family, milk-white, very sturdy and well conducted, with its demure blossoms arranged in tidy clusters on silver stems. Even if you are not making a grey border it is worthy of a place in the garden. There are very few white flowers that last, as this one does, for weeks after they have been cut. Moreover, it has none of the rather artificial appearance of most of the immortelles; it shines as fresh as any daisy in the meadows; and it isn't till you run your fingers over the blossoms, and hear them rustle like tissue paper, that you realize it may be a great deal older than it looks.

When we turn to I, we have to keep a tight rein on the superlatives . . .

Convolvulus Cneorum. This is a flower of jade and moonlight. The leaves, with an undercoat of silver, might be twining round the stem of a Chinese vase; the flowers are white trumpets, but the petals are of a finer material than the homespun hedge convolvulus, and seem to be cut from Chinese silk. The only reason why this exquisite flower is not the cause of exceptional swoonings from our visitors is because it seldom produces more than three or four blossoms at a time. In all this carolling of silver some people might miss it altogether.

This brings me to our final category, which I have linked together under the genus . . .

Bendingdowners. You will not find this word in any botanical dictionary, but it seems to me to fill a long-felt want, because of the extremely large number of flowers such as snowdrops, whose beauty cannot be properly appreciated unless one's body is in a position where the head is measurably lower than the sit-upon. There are three very precious little Bendingdowners in our border, marked J, K, and L. They are *Artemisia pedemontana*, *Achillea argentea*, and *Diotis candidissima*.

I will not weary the reader with any more of these journalistic prose poems. I will merely say that they all have the beauty of plants that have been silvered with hoar-frost, and if on occasions they are responsible for giving you a crick in the back, you will not—if you have a soul—complain.

PRACTICAL NOTE

Those who have ploughed through the foregoing pages will, I hope, have formed a picture of opulence, elegance and luxuriance. (If they have been able to form any picture at all!) But I hope even more earnestly that they will not have gathered the impression that such a picture can only be painted at the cost of a great deal of trouble, labour and expense.

On the contrary. Of all the borders I have ever made, the grey border has been the cheapest to establish and the easiest to maintain. Let us give chapter and verse for this contention. *Watering*. The first border was planted in the spring of 1964, which heralded the longest, dryest, hottest and sunniest summer within living memory. By the middle of August most of England's lawns had their tongues hanging out, so to speak, and even in the shadiest forests the leaves of the rhododendrons were parched and drooping. But apart from the first fortnight or so, after the plants were bedded out, the border received no water whatsoever. It just didn't want it. And yet, it faces due west, and from the middle of the afternoon is in full sunlight.

Weeding. We have already noted the exceptionally rapid growth of many grey plants. As a result of this growth, within a very short period we have a ground cover which smothers any weeds rash enough to attempt to establish themselves. From the end of July onwards weeding stops altogether. Obviously, this almost tropical proliferation has its drawbacks, but they are not as severe as one might imagine; for though some of the more delicate Bendingdowners are apt to be smothered, ten minutes with the secateurs will soon put that right.

Staking. Mr Page is a prize staker. Sometimes I suspect that he would stake the daffodils if he had the time, though he always stakes with such cunning that you never realize that there are any stakes at all. But in the grey border he has been able to keep his staking down to a minimum.

Hardiness. I am afraid that we must face the fact that the greater part of a grey border, to achieve its full spectacular effect, must be planted afresh every spring. Obviously there are exceptions, such as the silver ivy which we mentioned earlier on, and a few of the plants might be regarded as border-line cases, which would probably pull through the winter if they were given some protection. However, even if they survived, they would be lank and straggly. It is far better to sow seeds, or take cuttings, if you have a cold greenhouse. (The majority of the grey plants seem to root from cuttings with exceptional speed.) Failing that, you will just have to buy plants every year. See appendix for the best source of supply.

Soil and Aspect. Considering their aristocratic appearance, grey and silver plants are exceptionally accommodating. They are tolerant of lime and though they will face up to full sunshine they will flourish in a moderate degree of shade. Needless to say, you could not grow them in a chalk pit, nor along a dark North wall where the sun never penetrated. And like most other plants—with certain rock-loving and wall-growing exceptions—they are grateful for a nice mulch well-rotted compost.

CHAPTER SEVEN

LETTER TO A GENTLEMAN IN A HIGH WIND

ALTHOUGH the principal task of the garden writer, unless he is to become an intolerable bore, must be to describe the pleasures of his craft, he would scarcely be worth his salt if he did not also, however reluctantly, describe the pains. In the last chapter we made passing reference to one of the principle sources of pain in the garden, which can be summed up in a single word—chalk. In the present chapter we shall consider another equally potent source of pain—wind. Indeed, we shall consider the two of them together. Chalk and wind are our two greatest enemies, and any gardener who has to fight both of them at once may well feel like giving up in despair.

He need not do so. Hence this letter.

Dear Jimmy,

You have been much in my thoughts in the past few days, perched in your eyrie on the bleak Sussex downs. Even in my comparatively sheltered retreat the winds have been alarming, sweeping across the common like a pack in full cry. Sometimes I feel that I am being personally torn up by the roots. What *you* must have been feeling I hardly dare to think.

And here comes your letter, confirming my worst suspicions. So you are going to give it all up—the garden of which we have so often talked and dreamed together —the garden to which, in a modest way, I have sometimes helped to contribute. After seven years of blood, tears, toil and sweat, the winds have finally got you down. And not only the winds, but the chalk. You thought that you had at last defeated it, or at least come to terms with it. You had learned that on a chalk soil there were many lovely plants that would always be denied to you, but you had also discovered, by much costly trial and error, that there were almost as many plants, of almost equal beauty, that you could grow with complete success. From these plants and shrubs you had contrived your garden, and you had given it vital shelter by broad belts of Scotch firs, that I loved so much. I have really no right to be wise after the event, for though you will remember that I expressed a doubt as to these trees' survival, I suggested nothing to take their place. Besides, during these seven years, the firs had seemed to be holding their own. True, they were rather battered, and their trunks were twisted, but they *were* growing, and as each year went by the shelter they gave was more substantial.

But now . . . I quote from your letter:

> The roots of the firs have got into the accursed chalk. The disaster you warned me about has happened. I'm afraid that they've had it. A dozen of them crashed down in the gale last week, leaving great gaps through which the wind is pouring like an angry sea. As for the rest of them, they're all turning yellow and the chap from the local nursery tells me that they're suffering from 'chlorosis' and that there's nothing to be done about it. Considering that he supplied them and planted them in the first place I think that he might have warned me before, but it's a bit late in the day to complain about that. So I give up. I just can't go on. Even if I could afford it I can't build walls all round the place. They'd have to be twenty feet high and it would be like living in a barracks. But without some sort of shelter the garden will just blow into the sea. So I quit, and my only consolation is that 'it was fun while it lasted'. For there *is* nothing that can be done about it, Beverley, is there? I am afraid I know all too well what your answer will be.

No Jimmy, you don't. My answer is that there is something very definite to be done. The rest of this chapter will be devoted to telling you and your fellow sufferers precisely what it is.

High up on the Sussex downs, facing due south towards

the unpredictable waters of the English Channel, there is a tall grey rambling house built in the year 1820 which is the home of a tall grey rambling gentleman born in the year 1884. I hope that Sir Frederick Stern, the gentleman in question, will not object to the description[1]; all great gardeners—and he is a great gardener—are also great ramblers; they spend the happiest and most significant days of their lives prowling and poking about and going round in circles. The pattern made by their footsteps is of infinite complexity and would probably make little sense to any but a devoted gardener, but by and large it is a pattern of happiness.

Round this rambling house the rambling gentleman, in the course of the last fifty years, has created a rambling garden which is one of the most remarkable gardens in the world. The most singular feature of it is provided by a vast chalk pit, in which the principal treasures are housed, sheltered from the winds of the north by a sheer white cliff and from the prevailing south-westerlies by a coppice of beech. When Sir Frederick first walked into this forbidding arena he can have had little idea of the horticultural battles that it was to witness; it must have seemed to him as though some titan had been slashing at the surface of the hills with a giant spade. Apart from the pit, on the other side of the house, on the rolling slopes that fall towards the sea, there are several acres of gardens that flourish with an equally surprising luxuriance. They have not been designed with any special care as far as 'landscaping' is concerned; they give the impression that they merely 'rambled' into existence, as though the plants and shrubs had themselves dictated the

---

[1] Sir Frederick, unhappily, is no longer with us, but since this narrative was written in his lifetime, I have left it unaltered.

shape they wished the garden to assume. This, indeed, is roughly what occurred.

I have called this one of the most remarkable gardens in the world. I will go further, and call it a magical garden. For two reasons:

The first reason why it is 'magical'—the adjective was not lightly chosen—is because it could not possibly have happened, but it did. If Sir Frederick ever thought of putting a motto over his front door he might do worse than choose 'Credo quia impossibile'. When a certain old nurseryman first saw the bleak, barren expanse of all that chalk with the white skin stretched over its bones, it repelled him. It was the kiss of death. And when young Mr Stern, as he then was, asked him what would grow on it, he shuddered and replied, 'Nothing at all.' An observation which might well have intimidated anybody but a fanatic, for the old nurseryman was no mean authority in the gardening world. To say that princes paled at his slightest word of command might be an exaggeration, but he certainly knew his stuff and he was not used to being flatly contradicted by amateurs.

This is what young Mr Stern proceeded to do for the next fifty years. On the site where 'nothing at all' would grow he planted, and went on planting, and though there were many heartbreaks and casualties, a great many things began to grow—plants and trees which scarcely anybody had ever dreamed of growing on chalk before. We will examine some of these plants and trees in greater detail, shortly.

And the second reason why this garden is 'magical'? Because of its whiteness, because of the canvas on which it is painted. One has gone through life looking at flowers against a dark background—the background of the good earth, in its various shades of brown and russet and tan and sepia.

And suddenly one finds these same flowers displayed against a totally improbable screen of white . . . drifts of anemones and daffodils dancing in a strange luminance, clusters of pale green hellebores lit by a radiance that seems to vibrate from the soil in which they are planted. The total effect is— to say the least of it—startling. It is as though a student of Rembrandt's portraits, schooled to study them in the customary sombre shades in which he shrouded them, were suddenly to see these same models disposed against a background of shining white.

I seem to have forgotten the title of this chapter. We called it 'Letter to a Gentleman in a High Wind' and it was addressed to 'Jimmy', who happens to be a real person, faced with a real problem. I promised to answer it.

The answer is to be seen in Sir Frederick's garden, in the shape of majestic groups of evergreen oaks—*Quercus Ilex*— which protect him, like giant sentinels, against the assaults of all winds and weathers. When I first stood under those oaks I could scarcely believe my eyes—or my ears—for at that very moment the wind was raging and snarling through their branches. Surely, I thought, they must have been planted a couple of centuries ago, in deep pits of imported soil, by some eccentric millionaire? Surely it was inconceivable that they could have come there of their own accord, and attained to such maturity, formed such an impregnable rampart, in the life span of a single man?

In fact, some of the largest of these trees *were* already in existence when young Mr Stern began his garden. But others were not, and they are almost as impressive.

And here is the vital heart of the matter, for those who,

like Jimmy, are condemned to inhabit these windswept, chalky deserts: *none of these trees has ever been staked, none of them has ever shown the least sign of chlorotic poisoning, and none has ever blown down, even in the cruellest gale.* To some readers this may not seem a matter of much consequence, to others— including myself—it will seem of very great importance. For often, when I was living in my previous garden, I walked up to the chalk hills after a night of storm, to be appalled by the slaughter of the beeches, which have the reputation of being happier on chalk than on any other soil. There they were, giants of the forest, laid low like so many ninepins, with their chalk-encrusted roots stretched tragically to the scurrying skies.

So there is the answer to your problem, my dear Jimmy: *Quercus Ilex*, the Evergreen Oak, sometimes called the Holm Oak. None of your stunted Scotch firs, none of your pathetic bulwarks of twisted thorn. And though I will not say 'none of your beeches', for the beech is a tree of exquisite beauty, in winter or in summer, you must be prepared, only too often, to bid it a sad farewell. The *Quercus Ilex* rises triumphantly above all these, sometimes to a height of eighty feet, *and it stays.* If you do not know it, and if you suspect that because of its toughness its appearance must be inelegant let me assure you to the contrary. It is of Mediterranean origin and in maturity is not unlike a giant olive.

And speaking of 'maturity', the *Quercus Ilex* is *not* a particularly slow grower. If you were ten years younger I would even suggest that you started a little plantation from a handful of acorns, which it produces in quantities during hot, dry summers; but perhaps that would be over-optimistic. All the same, you need not buy trees taller than two feet, and you need not cosset them with peat or manure. Simply fork up the chalk around them, give them a stake, if you must, for a couple of years, and a refreshing mulch from time to time, and leave them to do the rest. They will grow to stretch their sheltering arms around your garden, and when your time comes you can gracefully expire in their shadow, blessing—I hope—the memory of my name.

And now for an even more powerful enemy—chalk.

Those readers who have followed me down various garden paths throughout the century—and I have reason to believe that there are still a few such persons extant, crouched in shelters along the warmest stretches of the south coast, hugging their shawls around them—may recall that throughout my gardening life I have had a deep-rooted aversion to chalk. As the years went by, this aversion assumed almost maniac proportions. In garden after garden—I had to struggle with chalk. Not, it is true, the bleak, uncompromising, 100 per cent chalk which faced Sir Frederick Stern, but enough chalk to slam the door on a thousand dreams. No rhododendrons, no azaleas, no blue poppies. No kalmias, no auratum lilies, and very few of the heaths. The list of impossibles seemed endless. Time and again, poring over the catalogues, I would come up against the sinister footnote, 'Will not tolerate lime'. And I would thrust aside the catalogue, and stalk out to the border, and begin scrabbling in the earth, picking out tiny specks of the white poison. But what was the use, in the end? However many specks you removed there were more underneath; the soil was tainted beyond any hope of redemption. Unless one concreted the whole garden and imported acid soil at a cost which would give even Mr Onassis to pause, one just had to give in, and wave a sad farewell to half the most beautiful flowers in nature.

If I had only known of Sir Frederick's garden, or read his book[1] about it, things might have been very different. I would never deliberately have chosen to live in a chalky district—no sensible gardener would make such a choice—but at least I should have been able to see the chalk in its proper proportions; it would have been a problem rather than a poison, a challenge rather than a sentence of death. And since in so many areas of Britain and America, and indeed the whole world, this problem is daily facing thousands of gardeners who are not equipped to cope with it, I thought it might be useful to make a list of flowers that will not only tolerate chalk, but rejoice in it.

This list has been compiled on a principle not normally employed in gardening literature; the classification is psychological rather than botanical; by which I mean that my main consideration has been the personality of the gardener rather than the personality of the plant.

Thus, the first section is headed:

For the Exhibitionist

In this group are included all those gardeners who like to make a splash, to enrage the neighbours and generally *épater le bourgeois*. If, for example, you see a giant yucca flaunting its exotic blossoms in the tiny front garden of a seaside house whose windows boast that Bed and Board are available, you may safely conclude that the landlady is an exhibitionist. (And probably a very good cook.) I can say this without any suggestion of reproach because I am something of an exhibitionist myself.

[1] *A Chalk Garden* by F. C. Stern (London: Thos Nelson, 1960).

ECHIUM X SCILLONIENSIS

EREMURUS ELWESII

STOLEN FROM WILEY McLAREN

JEFFERSONIA DUBIA

HELLEBORUS X STERNII

E

Of all the chalk flowers that are calculated to draw the crowds I would put first:

Echium x scilloniensis. There is a fantastic photograph of one of these echiums in Sir Frederick's book which shows it towering over him to a height of about thirteen feet. He is looking up at it with an expression of mild astonishment, as indeed he may, because it is more of a tree than a flower. If you will glance at the illustration you will see that the leaves at the base are not unlike those of a palm, and that the whole thing resembles a monstrous red-hot poker. The flowers of this particular echium are of a pleasant shade of forget-me-not blue, but they also come in rose and lavender.

An exhibitionist's flower, you will agree, and maybe not everybody's cup of tea. Heaven alone can tell what a professional flower decorator would do to it if she ever got her hands on it for the purpose of floral decorations; she would need a container the size of the Albert Memorial.[1].

But there are smaller and more delicate echiums that you should know of—dwarf hybrids in translucent shades of pink and lavender; and though they may not fully satisfy the exhibitionist appetite they are still unusual enough to arouse curiosity. They all rejoice in chalk, and you will find a note in the appendix about growing them from seed.

The name 'echium', by the way, derives from the Greek word *echis*, a viper. If Marius were with us we might settle the long-standing argument as to whether the flowers were so called because the seeds resembled a viper's head or because the leaves were supposed to be a remedy for the adder's bite.

[1] Since these words were written I have learned that the echium illustrated in Sir Frederick's book has, alas. died. Apparently, it will not stand more than eight to ten degrees of frost. Even so, I shall 'stet' it. If one is not an optimist in this gardening game, one is nothing.

Still for the exhibitionist:

Eremurus, in numerous varieties. This is another titan, ranging itself in six-foot battalions, like soldiers in fancy-dress uniforms of pink and lemon and apricot and pure white. It is difficult to know with which flower to compare it, but from a distance a group of them might be mistaken for giant foxgloves. (The popular name for it, the Foxtail Lily, gives a clue to its appearance.) Of all the eremurus the most attractive are the Highdown hybrids, which were raised by Sir Frederick himself. They come very easily from seed and you will find all the necessary details about them in the appendix.

There are many other 'spectaculars' that we might mention, such as the *Lilium centifolium*, which may well reach a height of seven feet. But let us proceed to our next 'psychological' classification and consider gardeners of a very different sort of temperament, to whom chalk flowers may make a special appeal.

For Persons Psychic, Eerie, and Inclined to Believe in Ghosts

Quite evidently this is not the sort of definition that you will find in the learned botanical journals, and it may need a word of explanation. So let us paint a picture. If you were to wander up the drive to Sir Frederick's house and creep into his garden, during any day from January to May, you would find yourself surrounded in the shadows by drifts of those flowers that—to me at any rate—will always be the ghost flowers of Nature's kingdom, the hellebores. Pale and wan, in every ethereal tint, from the waxen innocence of the Christmas Rose to the exquisite decadence of the *Helleborus foetidus*. Floral anthropomorphism is a habit to be discouraged in serious gardening, but is it so wrong to see flowers as people and people as flowers? Wrong or right, this is a habit from which I cannot disengage myself. And really, it is not so wildly fanciful to see the hellebores as ghost flowers. They seek the shadows, they are creatures of the dark days when the winds sigh through the bare branches; and—alas—when you bring them into the house, and surround them with the warmth of human companionship, they swoon and fade away.

Everybody knows the Christmas Rose, *Helleborus niger*, and most people know the common forms of the other hellebores, which bear the pretty country name of Lenten Lilies. However, comparatively few people are aware that the hellebore family come arrayed in so many dresses, pale jade flushed with purple, deep chocolate, pale pink flounced with leaves of marbled green.

All of them thrive in chalk. Why not? They are ghost flowers—at least, that is my contention—and it is only proper that they should thrive on an ectoplasmic diet.

Now for the next psychological classification . . .

For Shrinkers

The Nichols theory of shrinking has already been fully explained so we need not go into it again. I mention it here merely in order to emphasize that if your space is limited, and if you are obliged to work with chalk, you may find yourself less conscious of its drawbacks in the rock-garden than in any other part of your domain.

There are dozens of miniature delights that lap up chalk as if it were their mother's milk. At the risk of sounding arbitrary I would give first place to . . .
Jeffersonia dubia. This is so pretty that it almost makes you laugh. (Do you ever find yourself bursting into a sort of lunatic laughter at the sheer prettiness of things?) Why it

should be called '*dubia*' I cannot imagine, because there is nothing in the least dubious about the delight of its pale lavender blossoms, which in shape recall the flower of the St John's Wort, and have a most endearing habit of coming up in thick clusters, as though they had been tied into formal bouquets. A certain mystery surrounds this small treasure. It so greatly appealed to me on my first acquaintance that when I got home I looked it up in a number of authorities— rather as one might look up a lady in de Brett, if one were in the habit of falling in love with peeresses. To my surprise all the experts insisted that the jeffersonia demanded peat, and shade, and sandy soil, and all the conditions that one normally associated with woodlands on an acid soil. The plain answer to this is that it doesn't. It performs, and performs exquisitely, on chalk.

And now the list of chalk-loving miniatures becomes formidable indeed; one is reminded of an audition at a musical, when bevies of young ladies wait in the wings, poised to flutter out and display their charms. At random I call out the name of . . .

Pulsatilla vulgaris (Syn. *Anemone pulsatilla*). These are scattered all over Sir Frederick's garden, where they seed themselves at random, often in the most unlikely places. If you are new to gardening the word 'anemone' may have a limited connotation. Either it will recall the drifts of wild white anemones in the woods where you played as a child, or it will bring to mind the rather gaudy bunches of red and blue *Anemone de Caen* that are offered by the florists in late winter, at half-a-crown a bunch. They come from Cornwall and I sometimes buy them, but usually regret having done so. Nine out of every dozen invariably flop, and the remaining three last forever.

The pulsatillas are a very different cup of tea. They come in deep violet, crimson and sheer white. They have the added charm of growing old gracefully; as soon as they have reached maturity they adorn themselves in the most elegant silver wigs, fashioned from the seed pods. When summer is gone, the wigs blow off with the first winds of winter, float far and wide, and eventually transform themselves into families of new pulsatillas. A more graceful method of perpetuating the species, you will agree, than is habitual among human beings.

A last word about the pulsatillas, from the pen of Sir Frederick himself, to show you what good clean prose a gardener writes when he cares to: 'Mice like them. We have watched a mouse come along and bite off a seed head and take it to its nest as a soft cushion for its young. The best time to move them is when they are in flower or just coming into flower.'

As we suggested above, the list of chalk-loving—or at least chalk-tolerating—miniatures is too extensive to enumerate in a volume such as this. The cyclamens and the baby daffodils, all the dwarf irises, the crocuses and tulips in every variety . . . to say nothing of such common but beautiful plants as the aubretias. And if any gardener felt an absolutely overwhelming urge for some treasure to which chalk is poison, he might allow himself a little pardonable deceit, by contriving pockets of acid soil which could be held in waterproof containers concealed in the earth. But he should remember that they *must* be waterproof—lime-hating plants are poisoned not merely by contact with the chalk *per se*, but by any water that has come into contact with it.

If you read Sir Frederick's book you will find that he has arranged his chapters to correspond with every month of the year. Each chapter is a bevy of blossom, from the snow-drops and the aconites of the shortest days, through the long glittering parade of the cherries and the crabs; the pæonies and the roses (his tree pæonies have to be seen to be believed) into the rich fires of autumn. (Many of the thorns, in my own experience, colour better on chalk than on a neutral soil. They also colour superbly, of course, on a very acid soil. They don't seem to like half-way-house conditions.)

And there we will leave the tall grey house set on the windswept hills, and the garden which 'could never have happened'. But it did happen, because one man was deter-mined that it should. If he could do it, so could you.

Postscript. In spite of the occasional ecstasies of this chapter it should not be taken to indicate that any gardener would be wise deliberately to choose a chalky environment. True, when I asked Sir Frederick if he had ever regretted his chalk pit he replied with a firm and vibrant 'No', and regarded me with an expression of challenge which in a less kindly personality might have been described as a glare, as though he expected me to contradict him. I certainly shall not ven-ture to do so, because the making of his garden has been an heroic achievement, and obviously he has enjoyed every moment of the battle. But it *has* been a battle, and most of us may feel that we have to fight enough battles in our pri-vate lives without seeking any more of them in our gardens.

Therefore, the would-be gardener who is free to make a choice should never choose chalk. However, vast numbers of people are not in such a happy position. The locality of their domicile is dictated by their jobs, their families, their relations, their health, their finances and a thousand-and-

one circumstances over which they have no control whatsoever. Whether they like it or not, they have to take their
chalk and lump it. These words have been written in the
hope that they may help such people to make the best—if
not of a bad job—at least of a very tricky one.

CHAPTER EIGHT

THE ENEMY WITHIN OUR GATES

A robin red breast in a cage
Puts all Heaven in a rage.

So wrote the poet Blake, and I could not agree with him more. Anything in a cage, animal or human, is an affront to the Almighty, with the possible exception of budgerigars who have the run of a large kitchen, or elderly parrots of expensive tastes who are encouraged to walk across the dining-room table in order that they may have their heads scratched while they are placated with hot-house grapes. Otherwise, every cage, and every bar of every prison-house should be chucked into the bottom of the deep blue sea.

119

In the matter of prisons for man or beast, whether located in Sing Sing or Regent's Park, I am an uncompromising anarchist and so, it would seem, was Blake. He it was who wrote, '*In standing waters we should look for poison.*' These words echo and re-echo with a tragic significance, conjuring up a vision of the standing waters of the soul, as it grows darker and colder in the prison cell, more foetid, more irrevocably tainted with the microbes of bitterness and despair.

And yet, as a footnote to Blake, I can still retort:

> A squirrel in a walnut tree
> Infuriates a man like me.

Which brings us to the whole problem of animals, pests, and the gardener. Not only one's own animals—the dogs who bury bones at the foot of the Regal Lilies and the kittens who powder their noses in the seed boxes—but those who arrive of their own accord, the rabbits who escape from the park in order to dine off the aubretias, the mice who nibble the crocuses, the sparrows who peck the cherry buds, the wild duck who streak across the skies like things from outer space and dive-bomb the pond, smack in the middle of a newly opening clump of water-lilies. Not to mention all the creepy-crawlies. I like to think that I am on friendly terms with the whole animal kingdom and that when one goes to heaven one will be constantly surrounded—indeed almost smothered—by furred and feathered creatures who will no longer be agitated by the fears that beset them on earth. But sometimes . . . well . . . I wonder.

This difficult question is all summed up by the squirrels in the walnut tree.

The walnut tree is the second largest tree in my garden and a most beautiful tree it is, especially on a clear winter's morning, when the strong musical design of the branches seems to sing against the cold blue sky. The pale grey bark, from a distance, has the quality of the skin of some gigantic serpent. According to the experts the tree is about 160 years old, and last year a wood merchant offered me £100 for it. I informed him that since the cottage was Crown Property we were not allowed to cut down any trees without the permission of the Queen, that if we did so we should be promptly clapped in the Tower, and that one of us, at least, would deserve to go there.

However, the walnut tree is not only beautiful but fruitful. In the first year it produced so many walnuts—small but very sweet—that our wrists ached with cracking them. But that was the only year in which we had any walnuts to eat. The word got round, the jungle telephone began to ring, and by the following summer the squirrels had realized that they were on to a good thing. They came from far and wide, and they have been coming ever since. They appear with uncanny regularity at the beginning of the second week in July, usually on a Sunday morning. One comes home from church, helps oneself to a glass of sherry, and steps into the garden, filled with amiable intentions, one's mind echoing to the magnificent phrases of the Benedicite. '*O ye Whales and all that move in the Waters, bless ye the Lord.*' This is my favourite verse; it conjures up a vision of schools of whales with balloons spouting out of their noses. On each balloon is written a pious injunction. The larger whales have quite a lot written on their balloons, the smaller whales have something short and simple, like 'Hosanna'. Let us hope that God has time to read them.

And then, straight from the heavens, there flutters a small and sinister object . . . a fragment of the green skin of a walnut. It lands on the path, telling its story all too clearly. The squirrels have arrived, precisely on time. It is really quite extraordinary, as though they kept diaries in which they wrote: 'Sunday July 9. Call on B.N. and inspect walnut trees.' At the moment there are only two of them, a sort of advance guard, flicking their tails in the swaying branches; and since they have not yet realized their strength, and still have some of the innate timidity of wild creatures, they scamper away at a clap of a hand, streaking from the walnut into the deeper recesses of the copper-beech, and from there into the pear tree, whence they disappear into one of the neighbouring gardens. But they will be back tomorrow, and the day after, in ever increasing numbers, and for weeks the lawns and the paths will be littered with scraps of shells and broken nuts, and the whole garden will look like Hampstead Heath after an exceptionally rowdy bank holiday.

Why this sends me almost mad with irritation I do not know. We have no real need of the walnuts, and though it is a bore to be woken up at dawn by a fusillade of hard objects clattering on to the roof of the woodshed one gets used to it in time. Perhaps the real reason for these feelings is hidden in some hard primitive residue of masculine aggressiveness and general beastliness. Some part of the subconscious is probably outraged by the realization that for once in a way the animals have the upper hand. They ignore the shouts and hand-clappings, they shrug off the windfalls that one throws into the branches, and they sit there, bobbing up and down in the breeze, so completely impervious to reproof that from time to time they seem to be aiming the nuts directly at one's head.

Pests and the gardener, what a puzzlement it all is! Especially if the gardener is something of a sentimentalist, in spite of the aforesaid residue of primitive masculine beastliness. One sees a woolly caterpillar having an expense-account luncheon off the leaves of a Super Star rose; and one's hard clever hands go out to squash it. And then, suddenly, one does not feel so hard or so clever, and one's fingers falter and a thousand moral problems present themselves. Here is this small furry creature, which has something faintly kittenish about it, and perhaps this may be the crowning moment of its life. It may be saying to itself, 'All is well, God's in His heaven and all's right with the world. The flavour of these leaves is delicious, I am storing up strength, and soon I shall be able to hurry back to Mrs C, bursting with vitality and glowing with hope . . . the hope that by the time summer comes we shall all be safely and gloriously attired in the dresses that Nature is keeping in store for us, fluttering over these roses in the guise of butterflies.'

And so, quite possibly, one leaves the caterpillar to get on with it, and walks away, buoyed up by the sort of moral superiority that gratifies the Jains, the Hindu sect who feel so strongly about taking the life of any living creature that they breathe through veils of gauze lest they should inadvertently swallow a gnat. However, this complacency is premature, because almost certainly before the day is out one will have visited the tool-shed to make sure that there is an adequate stock of poisonous insecticides with which to deal with the problem.

In this caterpillar business, or indeed in the whole matter of pest control, the ultra-sensitive person will agree that poisoning is much kinder than squashing—to the poisoner. It is death at one stage removed, an anonymous scientific sort of death for which he feels no personal responsibility.

There is only one drawback to it. As he poisons the leaf which will eventually poison the caterpillar, the poisoner also happens to be poisoning himself.

No doubt it was only fancy that made me think that as those last words were being written a shadow passed across the lawn, over all the lawns of the world, in the past few years, at an open window and sometimes the garden seems to take control. Be that as it may, a shadow *has* been passing over the lawn, over all the lawns of the world, in the past few years, and as each year goes by it grows just a little darker and spreads just a little wider. Most gardeners, if they are aware of it at all, try to forget about it, turn their heads and walk away. Others do not find it so easy to forget. We are obsessed with a sense of guilt, as though in our carelessness we had forgotten to lock the gate, and had found on the following morning that something had got in during the night. Something that we could not see, lurking in the background, biding its time. Something hostile, and intrinsically evil.

This 'something' is poison, in one of the myriad forms in which mankind—and particularly the gardening community—is spreading it over the surface of the earth in order to combat the various pests which prey on plant life. That phrase—'particularly the gardening community'—may strike the reader as uncalled for, if not faintly ridiculous. Obviously neither Mr Smith, as he sprays his roses in a suburban garden, nor Mrs Jones, as she sprinkles her weed-killer over a patch of crazy paving, can be poisoning the earth's surface to a degree that is in any way comparable with the governments who send out their helicopters to shed a rain of death over thousands of miles in the space of a single afternoon. But if we multiply Mr Smith and Mrs Jones by their millions and their tens of millions, as we must do if we have any regard for world statistics, we must concede that we are 'all in it'; we cannot evade a modicum of personal responsibility. The object of the next few pages is to enquire what the average gardener can do about it, if he can do anything at all.

In my own case it was a book which first opened my eyes to the reality of this shadow creeping towards us. The book, as some readers may already have guessed, was *The Silent Spring* by Rachel Carson, which is certainly one of the outstanding books of the twentieth century, or indeed, of any century. I had the honour to meet its author not long ago in New York City and I am not likely to forget the experience. Imagine an apartment of great luxury, with tall windows through which the façade of sky-scrapers shone like a backcloth of spangled gauze. Imagine a crowd of rich women clothed almost exclusively in mink, so that if one half-closed one's eyes they gave the impression of a single, immense furred animal sprawled across the polished floor. And then try to see this little woman, in an ill-fitting woollen dress, facing them and talking to them, in a voice that rose scarcely above a whisper, about 'clouds of death' enveloping us in a curtain more lethal than any that has yet been woven by the atom bomb, and 'rivers of destruction' causing a wider and more lasting havoc than any natural torrents that have yet riven the earth's surface. The phrases were sensational, and although it was a woman who was speaking to us, a shy, diffident and very feminine little person, she spoke with the authority of a scientist whose record is as distinguished as that of any of her contemporaries in the Northern Hemisphere.

The theme of *Silent Spring* is implicit in its title, conjuring up as it does the grim picture of tracts of the earth which will soon be so poisoned by the mass use of various forms of chemical insecticide that all bird life will have vanished and the air will be robbed of its natural music. Such areas are in fact already in existence and are increasing at an alarming speed. Behind this theme lies the author's passionate conviction that the delicate balance of Nature, the exquisite spider's-web equilibrium on which life is sustained, can only be disturbed at our gravest peril, and that we are not only disturbing it but disrupting, and on our way to destroying, it, beyond repair. This tremendous indictment is sustained throughout the book by an array of facts which have not been seriously challenged, except—not unnaturally—by certain of the vested interests of the great chemical combines. It would be far beyond the scope of this small book to attempt a précis of these facts, and my main purpose in writing about *Silent Spring* at such length is to persuade people to read it.

And, of course, to ask the question, 'What are we going to do about it . . . we, the average gardeners, going about our small plots, dealing death in our modest little doses?'

Let us study the death cycle through the medium of one of the systemic insecticides which I have personally used and recommended. We will call it X. (Systemic insecticides are, of course, solutions that are fed into the roots and carried into the entire system of the plant, where they are fatal to those forms of insect life which absorb them.)

In my own garden we first used X to destroy greenfly on roses. It was so spectactularly effective that, for the first time in my life, I had a garden that was totally free from the pest;

the leaves of the roses looked as though they had been washed and polished by hand; even the creepers, high up near the roof, were immaculately clean. It was equally effective, we discovered, in dealing with the ubiquitous caterpillar. For two years, a group of Japanese maples had been regularly stripped of their leaves; by June they always looked as though they had been attacked by a plague of locusts. A single application of X, in the third year, disposed of this problem for good. The maples were as immaculate as the roses. And it was all so simple! No tiresome spraying, no bending down to get at the underside of the leaves . . . simply a few teaspoonfuls in a watering can.

Then *Silent Spring* came into the house, and somehow we began to feel that these bright green leaves did not look quite so pretty. For we realized that the various insects which were absorbing these poisons were being transformed into 'carriers'; they were not merely vanishing into thin air, they were being absorbed by other insects and, of course, by the birds, who became 'carriers' on a wider scale, for it is the nature of some poisons to accumulate malignant residues in the body. And yet again through the birds, as they flutter to the earth when their day is done, to the rodents—the classic conductors of plague throughout the centuries. To say nothing of the vast apparatus of modern sewerage, the 'bowels' of the modern industrial state, through which the poisons seep to the seas around us, to be absorbed by the fish, and eventually returned to the earth for human consumption. I am incompetent to describe with scientific accuracy the various links in the chain—however tenuous and indi-vidually minute—which leads from the spouts of our own watering cans to the food on our own tables, and to the tables of our neighbours. But that it exists there is no doubt whatsoever, and every day brings fresh evidence of it in the national press, for those who have eyes to read. One of the most distressing was the recent mass death of hundreds of cats and dogs who had eaten a pet food manufactured from horses who had grazed in fields which were directly affected by these poisons. Perhaps some of the people who heaved a small sigh for those unhappy creatures might have been more gravely disturbed if they had known that it is only a short step from the poisoning of animals to the poisoning of human beings.

Once again . . . what are we going to do about it?

This is what we did in our own garden. Precious little it was, but at least it was an effort.

Sickened by this accumulation of poisons—the shelves of the tool-shed were beginning to suggest a miniature armoury of chemical warfare—we decided to call a halt and see what could be done by other methods. We chose as the subject of experiment a clump of caryopteris, the exquisite hardy shrub which paints the October borders with drifts of Botticelli blue. I had sung the praises of this flower in another book, and sometimes visitors who had read about it were anxious to see it for themselves. However, all we had to show them was a mass of brownish crinkled leaves, for the caryopteris is especially prone to attack from thrips. Now the obvious modern antidote to thrips is D.D.T., but since D.D.T. in some form or another is one of the principal causes of the world's toxic condition we virtuously ignored it and went back to the old-fashioned extract of Pyrethrum.

Every day for the next fortnight we anxiously watched the caryopteris to see if the Pyrethrum was taking effect. We had high hopes, for Pyrethrum, after all, is an old-fashioned remedy that has proved its efficacy over the years. But as the days went by we began to suspect that our particular brand of thrips had a special toughness; maybe they had learned a thing or two, maybe the fact that their forebears had been subjected to the greater rigours of D.D.T. had given them some sort of immunity against the milder assaults of Pyrethrum. Whatever the cause, it was evident by the end of the week that the Pyrethrum was having no effect whatsoever. And though we sprayed again, and yet again—spending roughly three times as much as if we had used D.D.T.—the thrips emerged triumphant.

So what is one to do, if one is not only a gardener but a responsible citizen who is not altogether bereft of imagination nor devoid of a social conscience?

This was the question I went on asking myself throughout the summer. 'It is monstrous,' I said to myself, 'that a beautiful thing like a garden should have to be turned into a sort of testing ground for Imperial Chemicals Ltd. Men have been gardening since the beginning of time and when Adam bit the first apple he didn't have to wipe it with a fig leaf in case the peel had been tainted with an arsenic spray.'

Some of the practical ways in which I tried to live up to these convictions were not, perhaps, so futile. Thus, when the lawn—our pride and joy—suddenly erupted into a miniature volcanic range of ants' nests, I did not use the ant-killing powder which lay in readiness in the tool-shed. That went into the dustbin. Instead I borrowed a beetle, with which I wrought instantaneous death over a wide area. My consolation in this savage business was the thought that if one were an ant one would probably choose this manner of being murdered in preference to dying of slow suffocation with one's small and delicate limbs encased in a patent product devised by man.

Again, when the lavender bushes became infested, as they always do, by the frog-hopper, which exudes its nasty spittle so lavishly that the whole plant becomes an object of repulsion, I did not employ the obvious remedy of D.D.T. I simply used the hose, bombarding the bushes with jets of pure water. The frog-hoppers came back again and again, but eventually they got bored and departed in disgust—presumably to spit with even greater fury in somebody else's garden.

And then there were long hours spent in hand-picking the leaves of various infected shrubs, and burning them, and gouging out the maggots that burrow into the new growth of the Scotch firs, and even trying to see what one could do with one's bare thumbs against red spider in the greenhouse . . . an occupation which Mr Page sadly but rightly informed me was not likely to be very effective.

Yet again, we tried to make more effective use of the naked eye—an organ which some gardeners are inclined to neglect. Here is an example. One of the prettiest 'passages' in the garden is lined with irregular clumps of hostas, those very rewarding plants which provide us with some of the handsomest foliage in nature. One day Mr Page buttonholed me, saying, 'I'd like you to come and see something.' He led me to the hostas and there, sure enough, I saw something—something quite disgusting. It was an enormous snail that had buried itself deep in the centre of a magnificent hosta and was gorging away to its heart's content. Because Mr Page has a keen eye he had been led to this creature by the slimy trail of its passage across the leaves.

This seemed a test case. It would have been quite easy to

go to the tool shed and select the appropriate lethal weapon from the poison armoury. We did no such thing. Instead we spent a whole morning hand-picking each of the hostas for the noxious intruders, dragging them out protesting, and crunching them on the path. This was one of the less fragrant interludes in the week's work. But it cleared the hostas and at least it saved the garden, and thereby the world, from one more dose of poison.

However, it was a losing battle. Little by little, we have been obliged to revert to the poisons, with their miraculous but sinister potency. True, we try to use them with dis-crimination; and we can always console ourselves with the thought that 'everybody's doing it' and that the toxicity of the world at large cannot be greatly affected, one way or another, by the condition of an acre of earth in the county of Surrey.

But it is a barren sort of consolation, for my acre must be multiplied by millions of acres in the charge of other gar-deners. And to these acres must be added the tens of millions of acres over which the governments of the world are spread-ing their daily fumes of death.

This is one of those problems to which there would seem to be no glib and facile answer. All that can be said with any certainty is that the world at large should be aware of it— and the gardening world in particular.

CHAPTER NINE

GONE WITH THE WIND

ONE DAY my friend Marius asked me when I was going to write another detective story.

'I don't know, Marius. There always seems so much else to do. Why do you ask?'

He lay back in the deck chair and stretched out his long elegant legs. His eyes were following the flight of a cluster of thistle-down that had blown over the wall from the Common. It drifted into the branches of the pear tree, whence it would eventually drift away again, to cause us all a great deal of trouble.

Then he said: 'Because I think that I have an idea for you. Your detective, I remember, was a gardener and his name was Mr Green. He struck me, by the way, as a very formidable old gentleman.'

'There were occasions when he rather frightened myself.'

'I wonder if he would have frightened you in the situation I have in mind. May we have a moment to discuss it?'

'We have the whole afternoon.'

'Good. Let us begin with the crime itself. Would you have any objection to arson?'

'It would make a pleasant change from the usual murder.'

'So I imagined. We will assume, then, that Mr Green is employed by an insurance company to investigate the destruction by fire, in highly suspicious circumstances, of some valuable property. Would you agree to an eighteenth-century mansion in the Palladian manner, situated on a remote stretch of the Irish coast?'

'Most certainly.'

'And as a cast, would you care for an impoverished Earl married to a beautiful woman twenty years his junior, and a dissolute son and heir with every sign of drug addiction?'

'They sound most promising.'

'Very well. Mr Green goes to Ireland, meets the family, and prowls about among the ruins, sifting the rubble and sniffing the ash. For the first few chapters, no doubt, you will be busily employed with the red herrings which you manufacture so skilfully.'

'Thank you.'

'Then—this will have to be towards the end of Part One—there comes a night when Mr Green makes his first discovery. I should like it to be by moonlight, with his small figure outlined against the gaunt skeleton of the old house. He bends down, takes out his magnifying glass, and picks a weed that has struggled up through the scorched earth.

Bends down again, picks up another weed. He folds them in a piece of tissue paper, places them in his wallet, straightens himself, stares at the moon, and blinks. I seem to recollect that you always made him blink when he was on the scent?'

'Quite. But why is he blinking now?'

'Perhaps you will guess if I tell you the names of the weeds. *Chamaenerion angustifolium* and *Senecio squalidus*.'

'I am none the wiser.'

'Mr Green was evidently a better botanist than his creator. The Rosebay Willow-Herb and the Oxford Ragwort.'

These names were familiar enough. 'But what is their conceivable connection with a case of arson?'

Marius chuckled. 'Perhaps I am experiencing the same sort of satisfaction that you feel when you are deluding the reader. Let me give you one more clue . . . the Mafia.'

'The Mafia? I give up.'

'I will explain. It is simple; at least, Mr Green seems to have thought so.'

Whereupon Marius gave me his 'exposition'. It was indeed entirely simple, and in spite of its ingenuity it is credible.

When Mr Green found those two weeds pushing through the scorched earth—the Rosebay Willow-Herb and the Oxford Ragwort—a shutter flicked back in his memory, reminding him that once he had seen them growing together on another occasion many years ago, at the end of the Great War, among the ruins of a bombed-out church in the City of London. He remembered too, as many older readers may remember, that always after the fire and fury of the battle these same plants had arrived to clothe the desolation with their humble flowers, as though Nature were covering the ugly wounds with a bandage of her own contriving. Since he had an enquiring mind, and was 'a

134

better botanist than his creator', he did some research, and discovered that these weeds had a special partiality for earth that had been burned. The original habitat of the Oxford Ragwort, whence it spread all over Europe, was *in the volcanic soil that stretches around the slopes of Mount Etna in Sicily, which is the home of the Mafia.*

And now, here is the trick that Marius had been keeping up his sleeve. The gardener in the ruined mansion was a Sicilian. In league, of course, with the dissolute, drug-taking son of the house, who was using the lonely beach as a centre for the sort of narcotics organization in which the Mafia specialize. The seeds of the plants—which, as it happens, are nowadays seldom found in Ireland—had been accidently carried in the turn-ups of the Sicilian's trousers.

However, as we have observed all too frequently before, we were supposed to be writing a gardening book. Besides, I really do not see why I should hand out free scenarios to my fellow novelists.

What are weeds? And how do they arrive in our gardens?

The prettiest definition of a weed that I ever read was coined by a learned director of Kew Gardens, Sir Edward Salisbury, who wrote, 'A weed is a flower in the wrong place.' Or, more generally, 'A plant growing where we do not want it.' This is not only a penetrating observation but a kindly one; it does not condemn a weed *per se*, it merely condemns the environment.

The second question, 'How do weeds arrive in our gardens?' is among the most exciting in the green pages of Nature. How many people are aware that large numbers of our own so-called 'native' plants were first introduced to

Britain by the legionaries of Caesar, marching through the dust of the Roman roads? In the words of the aforesaid learned curator, 'The Roman military sandal, which was studded with hobnails under the margin, the toe and the heel, would have formed a most effective temporary catchment in the dispersal of the seeds of weeds and aliens.'[1] If we switch the clock forward a couple of thousand years we shall realize that today there are methods of distribution even more dramatic, such as through the slots in the rubber wheels of an aircraft, particularly if it had been obliged to make a forced landing in some foreign field. Were our friend Mr Green to allow his imagination a little scope, he would find a hundred ingenious plots and counter-plots hidden in the core of a single seed.

Moreover, as he ventured more deeply into the subject—the embryology of botany—he would become more and more impressed by the ingenuity which Nature displays in the function of reproducing herself, and by the toughness which she has developed to ensure that her fertility is not impaired. Did you know that if you are planning a raspberry bed in your kitchen garden, *all you have to do is to plant a pot of raspberry jam*? Put like that it sounds incredible and faintly ridiculous, and I have of course deliberately exaggerated the phenomenon. All the same, it is a well-established fact that seeds of both raspberries and blackberries have frequently germinated from the boiled pulp thrown on to the earth after the making of raspberry and blackberry jelly.

As for the mechanical methods which Nature has contrived in order to spread her progeny, these are so numerous and so complicated that if they had been invented by human beings they would have involved the issue of thousands of

[1] *Weeds and Aliens* by Sir Edward Salisbury (London: William Collins, 1961).

special patents. Among these perhaps the most remarkable might be concerned with the various ballistic devices of such plants as the Hairy Bitter-Cress, whose pods are literally 'explosive'. The slightest touch of a pod that is fully ripe sets off a chain of violent reactions in which elastic tissues are ruptured and coils are unwound with such force that the seeds are propelled, as from a super-catapult, to a distance of several feet from the parent plant. But this is as nothing to the spread of such seeds as the Canadian Fleabane, which is accomplished by a built-in 'parachute' comparing favourably with anything invented by man.

As if this were not enough, Nature has endowed some of her seeds with an astonishing life-span of fertility. When the huge seeds of the Egyptian Lotus were dug up from the peat-beds of Manchuria 80 per cent of them were found to be viable after lying dormant for over a thousand years. (The popular legend of wheat germinating from seeds found in the tomb of Tutankhamen was recently proved to be a journalistic invention.) A thousand years of viability, needless to say, is exceptional, but there are many seeds whose period of viability exceeds the normal life-span of human beings.

PRACTICAL NOTE

The fact that some seeds remain fertile for so many years should not encourage the idea that all seeds can be stored for an indefinite length of time. By and large we should follow the practice of Nature, who scatters her seeds to the earth as soon as they are ripe, and leaves the rest of the job to the sun and the rain. Indeed, some seeds, such as primulas, seem to germinate most freely if they are sown *before* they are fully ripe.

We suggested above that weeds are 'flowers in the wrong place' and we noted the remarkable ingenuity of the devices which Nature has contrived for their distribution.

We are now faced with a question of some importance, a question which most gardeners seem inclined to dodge. If weeds are indeed flowers, and often very beautiful flowers, are we justified in excluding them from the garden scene? Does not the very fact that we do so argue a regrettable lack of imagination? Consider the Lesser Celandines, whose exquisite little flowers greet the advent of spring only a couple of weeks later than the winter aconites. We gladly pay forty shillings a hundred for the aconites, and indeed no money could be more sensible invested. And when they dance into our lives, their small urchin faces greeting the sunshine with a golden grin, our hearts are lifted within us. But when the celandines come trooping in their train, shining with an even brighter gold, we scowl at them—at least, most people do—and get out a trowel and dig them up and throw them on the rubbish heap.

Why?

This question seems to me of real importance because it compels us to look not only at the 'weeds' but at *ourselves*; it forces us to examine our whole sense of aesthetic values; it obliges us to ask whether we still have that 'innocence of eye' which is the essential of all artistic perception—the direct vision, unsullied by snobbery or fashion or tradition, which makes us instantly respond to the brilliant beauty of a spray of bramble in an autumn hedgerow or the fantastic delicacy of the designs of duck-weed spangling a muddy pond.

However, there is no need to go to extremes about all this and I hope that the reader will not find in these theories any suggestion that he should throw out his arms in an ecstatic gesture to welcome every wild thing that seeks refuge in his garden. We must keep a sense of proportion, and admit, however reluctantly, that there are some wild flowers so virile and so prolific that we must beware of them, in spite of their beauty, for the simple reason that if we admit them they will end up by eating us out of house and home. Of all these, among the most dangerous are in the following class: *Plants that Seed Themselves in Walls*. Any beginner who has the luck to come into possession of a walled garden will very soon come to see his walls as canvases on which he can paint charming pictures. At first he will be content to adorn them with roses and clematis and wisteria, but as time goes by he will grow more ambitious; he will realize that these walls are potential 'hanging gardens', not necessarily of Babylonian proportions, but none the less delightful for their limitations. On them, as though he were nailing little pictures round his sitting-room, he can suspend pleasing patches of pink and mauve and white—aubretias and sedums and snow-in-summer.

Then Nature comes along in the shape, let us say, of a seed of that very pretty plant the Red Valerian, which may have been borne on the wind or—less poetically—ejected from the otherwise innocent posterior of a pigeon. Whatever its means of transport the valerian takes root in the crevices, sends out its shrill green leaves, and eventually bursts into song in a series of rosy arias round about the first week in July. And the garden will delight in this floral music, and so will its feline neighbours, for whom its aroma has always had a special appeal.

And it will go on delighting until one day, with a loud crash, the wall falls down.

Needless to say, it will not fall down as dramatically as all

that. But from the very first moment the valerian takes root, the wall is doomed. Unless you have actually seen the strength and persistence of this plant, thrusting deeper and deeper, displacing the mortar, lifting the bricks with a relentless pressure, you would not believe that it could do so much damage. Well, I have seen it in my own garden. I thought that we might allow just one clump of the pretty thing, providing that we watched it and did not let it get out of hand. But it was too quick for us, and too resistant, and in the end we had to rebuild a sizable section of the wall at a cost of nearly thirty pounds.

Another menace, all the more dangerous because it is so pretty, is the *Corydalis lutea*. There must be many thousands of gardens, particularly in the southern counties, where this charming little intruder has been welcomed with open arms. When it makes its first appearance you might well mistake it for a sort of maidenhair fern, so delicate and feathery are its leaves. Then the flowers come, pale yellow and shaped like those of a veitch, and for several weeks it is a joy. But do not let it fool you; this frail creature is even tougher than the valerian, and unless you are ruthless with it, your wall will start to crumble and eventually have to be rebuilt.

The strength of these weeds, their swiftness and their

cunning, is so formidable that while I was writing about them I could not help thinking how useful they would have been in a floral assault on Jericho. Instead of that rather vulgar business with the trumpets the affair could have been concluded far more gracefully with a handful of seeds.

Does this mean that there are no wild flowers to which the gardener may offer hospitality on his walls? No—and in a moment we will suggest a few that are not only charming but innocuous. But first, the time has come for a . . .

PRACTICAL NOTE

The methods by which we deal with wall weeds depend, of course, on the extent to which they have established themselves. Plants such as Red Valerian and *Corydalis lutea* can still be treated, in the second year of their growth, by local applications of weed-killer at double or treble strength. (Non-poisonous, if you please!) I usually do this by means of a small watering-can with a very narrow spout that can be pushed into the cracks.

But if the gardener buys a property where such weeds have been allowed to grow unchecked, or if he has himself neglected to control them, this method is inadequate. No amount of old-fashioned 'weed-killer', even at full strength, will have more than a temporary affect. This is where we have recourse to one of the hormone weed-killers which destroy plant life by absorption through the leaves. It is a slow and rather boring business; each leaf and stalk has to be carefully painted, and several applications may be necessary. But it does work in the end, as I have proved in the case of a sycamore seedling which was beginning to grow into such a hefty young tree that if it had been left for another year it would have done very grave damage.

Failing this procedure I know of nothing that you can do except to attack the wall with a pick-axe, collect the roots of the weeds, burn them, and telephone to the local builder.

And now for the list of those 'weeds' with which we might well enrich our own gardens, always remembering that because they are wild flowers, with an extra toughness and virility, they will need to be constantly watched and disciplined. We might compare them with slum children who are invited by some charitable hostess to join in a party for the children of the nobility and gentry. (Though I have usually found, on such occasions, that the children of the slums behave rather better than the children of Mayfair.)

Let us begin with an illustration from my own garden. During the summer months people wandering round the borders enquire the name of a delicate little plant which grows in drifts of pale lilac in all sorts of odd corners that might otherwise be barren.

'Is it a sort of thalictrum?'

'No, as you can see for yourself if you look more closely.'

They bend down and observe that the tiny flowers, which clothe the supple stalks in great abundance, are of the snapdragon family.

'Then what is it?'

'The name is *Linaria purpurea*.'

'Can one get it from the average nurseryman?'

'I very much doubt it.'

The reaction to this information depends on the sex of the visitor. The women are apt to sigh and cast wistful glances, the men are inclined to snort. After this, they usually ask where I got it myself.

'From the edge of a stream in a Wiltshire water-meadow. You have probably heard of it by its popular name of Purple Toad-Flax.'

'But surely . . . isn't that a *weed*?'

'Certainly it is a weed. But it is also a very pretty flower, don't you think?'

'Oh yes, I suppose it's pretty, all right. But well—a weed —I mean to say . . .'

There the dialogue usually stops, and what the visitor 'means to say' I have never understood. Nor does it greatly matter, for the little linaria is an invaluable addition to the summer border. It springs up in all sorts of odd corners, flowers from June till late October, and though it is thickly starred with blossom it is never obtrusive. One might say that it 'knew its place'. If it strays into areas where it is not wanted, it could not be easier to get rid of—a gentle tug, and the whole plant comes out, with no sign of protest.

Here is another:

Meconopsis cambrica (Welsh Poppy). If I were to ask you to imagine a blue poppy and then to paint it yellow, you might pardonably be puzzled. The reason for mentioning the blue poppy is because this supremely beautiful flower is beyond so many people's reach, and because in the yellow poppy they might find a sort of consolation.

We seem to be tying ourselves up in knots, so let us start again.

There must be thousands of people who have wandered through places like the Savill Gardens, where the blue poppies seem to be bluer and bigger and poppier than in any part of the world except their native Thibet. As they have wandered, they have been depressed by the thought that they will never be able to grow them like this, because they will never have such ideal conditions—shelter, moisture, semi-shade, a gentle slope, and super-acidity. This is where the wild yellow poppy might come dancing on to the stage of their imagination, like a good fairy in a pantomime. Because this is a *shade* poppy which is far less fussy, and far more robust, than its appearance would suggest. I have even seen it holding its own against clumps of 'dead' nettles in a wood in Westmorland.

This is a difficult list to compile, not only because of the vast extent of our native flora but because its practical application must depend so largely on the part of the country where the reader may happen to live. Perhaps the happiest of all the hunting grounds, if you are in search of rarities, lie in the marshy lands. Within a few miles of London you can still find the wild yellow iris *Iris Pseudacorus* growing in profusion. Along the banks of some of the streams that meander through the Wiltshire water meadows these irises grow so thickly that a local farmer told me he wouldn't care if I removed a whole cartload of them. In Norfolk you can still find the fascinating Marsh Helieborine, though on no account should you disturb it; not only is it getting scarce, but it would almost certainly die on you. The same applies to the Marsh Orchid *Orchis strictifolia* which once flowered so freely in some parts of Suffolk that in August the little village boys used to stand in the lanes selling them at sixpence a bunch. To reproduce in the average garden the wild conditions which such a flower demands would be well-nigh impossible.

Finally, a naturalized wild flower which should be in everybody's garden . . .

Mimulus guttatus (Monkey Flower). This is buttercup yellow, nine inches high, splodged with brown, and as gay as they come. Why anybody ever called it a monkey flower is something of a mystery; if we were in search of an animal metaphor I would have settled for a sort of mad yellow spaniel, with its tongue hanging out. It grows in shadow or in sunlight, in damp soil or in dry and once it has decided that you are a friend, you will never get rid of it. Nor will you wish to do so.

My own mimulus was growing in a ditch in Gloucester-
shire when I was held up in a traffic block, and it put out its
tongue with such charming impertinence that I went over
and scooped it up. (It was one of hundreds that were so
closely crowded together that they were getting on each
other's nerves.) It has flourished exceedingly and its off-
spring have been distributed to many friends. This sort of
conduct can scarcely be described as 'vandalism'. But if any
members of the Wild Flower Protection League had been
present at the time they would probably have disapproved.

PRACTICAL NOTE (1)

After this bucolic interlude I almost hate to mention that
seeds of the *Mimulus guttatus* may be bought from a number
of nurserymen for a shilling a packet. 'So it isn't a wild
flower at all?' you may protest. The more indignant the
protest, the better I shall be pleased. The whole purpose of
this argument is to point out the folly of this arbitrary distinction between 'weeds', wild flowers, and garden flowers.
On some part or other of the earth's surface *all* flowers sown
by nature rather than by man could be condemned as
'weeds', if you are so inclined. In Darjeeling white orchids
grow 'like weeds', festooning the ancient branches of the
forests with their luminous petals, as though they were
hanging out flags for some ghostly festival. Would the people
who purse their lips when they see my drifts of toad-flax
disapprove of those orchids, simply because they are wild?
Would they proceed to tear them down, and plant little
packets of nasturtiums in their place? I would not put it
past them. Because, you see, they paid a shilling for the
nasturtiums, whereas the orchids were sent by God, and
something for which one has paid a shilling must, *ipso facto*,

be more desirable than something which has been bestowed by the Creator of the Universe.

Such people will have no interest in this brief list of weeds, merely because they cannot bring themselves to believe that anything can be of value unless it has been paid for in cash. But there may be others who will be encouraged to look at these flowers with a fresh eye, and through them to enter into a new world of beauty, with quiet colours and gentle rhythms and its own special poetry . . . the sort of poetry which inspired Meredith's 'Love in the Valley':

> Yellow with bird-foot trefoil are the grass-glades;
> Yellow with cinquefoil of the dew-gray leaf:
> Yellow with stonecrop; the moss-mounds are yellow;
> Blue-neck'd the wheat sways, yellowing to the sheaf.

PRACTICAL NOTE (II)

The word 'practical' may not be justified in this connection, for here I wish to ask a question rather than record a fact. The question is: 'If we bring wild flowers into our gardens, and if we give them special treatment, cosseting them, protecting them, and feeding them with the occasional unaccustomed luxury of a fertilizer, might we expect that in time they would grow larger and more luxuriant, until they could compete with their more sophisticated neighbours?' This is obviously an amateur question, but then I have never pretended to be anything but an amateur. I have a special reason for asking it. The most expensive single plant in my garden is a two-guinea specimen of the exotic *Orchis elata*, which occupies a V.I.P. position in the shade of the copper-beech, and causes gasps of astonishment from all who see it during its six-week flowering period from June to mid-July. Although it hails from Algeria, it is really only a sort of giant edition of the common Southern Marsh Orchid *Dactylorchis praetermissa* which grows so abundantly in British fields.

Supposing that we procured some of the 'common' orchids, planted them in the same sort of soil as they need in Algeria, and protected them with cloches during the winter, is there any chance that they might eventually develop into elatas and that after a year or two I might find myself in possession of hundreds of plants worth two guineas apiece? The answer is almost certainly 'No'.

CHAPTER TEN

THE MUSIC AND THE ROSES

As a frustrated composer I have always regarded gardens in terms of music, and it is perhaps significant that the people who have been kindest about the few gardens I have been able to design have been musicians. When the late Sir Thomas Beecham stepped on to the lawn at Merry Hall and walked towards the water garden, on a magical evening in June when the balustrades were garlanded in white roses, he exclaimed, 'This is sheer Mozart!' which was charming of him, but somewhat flattering. For there was a lot of blight on the roses, and it will be generally agreed that there was never much blight on Mozart.

To say that one regards a garden 'in terms of music' is not as airy-fairy as it may sound. If one's primary impulses in life are musical, if tragedy presents itself as a series of minor chords, echoing through some remote corner of the brain, if 'beauty' is seen as a series of melodic lines, whether they be the lines of a landscape or the sweeping curves of a sea-gull's wings—if all moments of emotion express themselves immediately and inevitably in their appropriate musical tempo, then one gives, or tries to give, a musical shape and content to the garden. How could it be otherwise? A blossoming apple tree is not merely a blossoming apple tree. It is an étude in D major, in six-eight time, scored mainly in the treble. And across the trunk, when one is contemplating it—particularly if an April breeze is alert among the branches—one mentally scribbles the mood in which the étude is to be played: *Allegro vivace*.

It is the same through the whole of one's gardening life, not only while the garden is being designed but in the after years, when at last there is time to wander in it and to seek its consolation. Each day suggests its appropriate composer; the key is set by the colours in the sky, the rhythm dictated by the wandering of the wind, and the general 'shape' by the seasons themselves. Thus, in the winter, Bach comes into his own, weaving fugues of extraordinary intricacy from the interlacing branches of the copper-beech. Bach wrote only forty-eight fugues on his well-tempered clavicord; I have written at least a hundred and forty-eight as I stare up into the beech on a January morning. Pure Bach it is—clean, austere, exquisitely mathematical, and always very near to God. Pattern upon pattern, line upon line, an unforgettable counterpoint of arboreal melody, etched in black against a sky of steel.

'This was a Delius day'. So begins an entry from one of my last year's diaries. There are many Delius days in the gardener's life, especially when the cuckoos are calling. They come in the spring and early summer, for Delius was essentially a composer of the green leaf and the sighing branch. To study one of his orchestral scores is to be reminded of the shifting play and interplay of the shadows from a willow tree, as it dreams over a lake.

And again . . . 'Ever since breakfast Beethoven has been making very ominous noises in the walnut tree'. The date of this entry is October the eleventh, and lest it should suggest irreverence for one of the greatest Titans who ever bestrode the world of man's emotions, I hasten to add that the walnut tree is one of the greatest that ever bestrode the acres of Ham Common. This tree is composed in the classical sonata form, with the trunk proclaiming the main motif, which is developed in a series of subsidiary themes through the upper branches. In the centre there is a beautiful adagio design, where the trunk and the branches part company. The final movement—the scherzo—is perhaps the most exciting of all, for it contains a number of dynamic passages for the percussion instruments, which are executed by our small but deeply dedicated orchestra of squirrels, hurling their nuts on to the roof of the tool-shed.

Beethoven would have loved my walnut tree and might well have written a masterpiece around it.

And again—time and again—'Chopin has been everywhere in the garden today'. Chopin, indeed, is our most frequent visitor, from the first snowdrop to the last leaf that drifts from the beeches on a winter's evening. The narcissi dance his mazurkas under the pear tree and throughout the summer his nocturnes echo over the lily pool. For every flower there is a Chopin étude, or perhaps I should say that for every étude there is a flower. And it is not only through the flowers that he speaks. On a June morning, when the spiders have hung the bushes with their silver webs, it is clear that they have been spending the night engaged less in spinning than in composing—creating a series of sparkling cadenzas as delicate and airy as the miraculous decorations that glisten on the pages of the *larghetto* in the F minor Concerto.

But how can all this be explained in terms of practical gardening?

Perhaps the best way to do so would be to consider the single example of the rose. I have been drawn into many heated arguments through my deep-rooted aversion to hybrid tea roses, which form the dominating feature of nine-tenths of the gardens of Britain and America. There are psychological reasons behind this aversion; these roses were the background to the gardens of my childhood, if a period of such violent storm and stress can be called a 'childhood' at all. (I have often wondered, with genuine curiosity, how it must feel for a child who can actually walk into his home without a feeling of terror, almost of panic, at the thought of what may be awaiting him inside.)

But this psychological complex is only the half of it; the aesthetic aversion is equally strong, and it is obviously so uncommon, and so unpopular, that I shall need a page or two to explain it. For to whisper a word against roses, in England or America, is simply not 'done'. When one suggests that we can have too many of them and that the role they are able to play in the garden is limited, one's remarks are received with the same sort of horrified incredulity as if one had observed, *en passant*, that all dogs were not necessarily the noblest creatures in the animal kingdom nor all babies the most beautiful examples of God's handiwork. This is the established legend among 'decent' people, and one cannot fight the establishment, even though a moment's honest reflection must reveal the fact that many dogs are not noticeably noble, and that most babies, to the impartial eye, are of considerable hideousness, with bald pates and lunatic expressions. Though obviously to be treated with kindness, they should be removed from the view of all but their parents for the first few months of their lives and kept, if possible, behind screens.

To the vast majority of the public, roses are above criticism. We are besotted by roses. We can no longer see them straight because of all the mist of sentimental tradition that has gathered round them. The rose has become a sort of moral status symbol. 'My love is like a red, red rose,' sang Burns, and for all the 100,000 members of the Rose Society this fits in very nicely with their personal predilections, evoking, as it does, a picture of a full-bosomed young lady with parted lips waiting to be wooed—but one hopes not too painfully scratched—against a background of Dorothy Perkins. If your adoration of roses is even faintly qualified there must be something morally wrong with you. For that matter, if your adoration of Burns is not whole-hearted you are similarly suspect. Well, I have never much cared for that greatly overrated poet and since reading the luridly scabrous verse which he scribbled for his private delectation I have cared even less.

Are there any other large groups of the public whom we can outrage, while we are about it? In the past few sentences we have presumably forfeited the sympathy of millions of garden-lovers, dog-lovers, baby-lovers and Burns-lovers all over the world. Perhaps that is enough to be going on with, for the moment.

All the same, sympathy or no sympathy, I trust that a few rose-lovers will read what follows. Whether they like it or not, they will perhaps agree that it has not often been said before.

In my own garden there are no hybrid teas, and the reason why there are none is fundamentally musical. There are roses in plenty on the walls, where they can dispose themselves in melodic lines, and there is a single Canary Bird weeping bush-rose by the lily-pool, because it has a musical 'shape'. But all the hybrid teas are banished to the annexe, in cutting beds. The flower of the rose, I need not be informed, is among the most beautiful objects on which the eye can rest, this side of the grave; but the bush itself is one of the ugliest. Before the reader dismisses this opinion as so much nonsense he might pause to ask himself why none of the great artists, from the Renaissance to the Impressionists, has ever painted one. There have been flower pictures by the thousand, in which roses play a supreme role, but never a picture, by any master, of a hybrid tea growing *in situ*.

Perhaps these very personal feelings may be easier to convey if we drop the metaphor of music and refer, in general terms, to Nature. Why should Nature approve of a hybrid tea? Without its flowers, which means for the greater part of its life, it is gaunt, gawky, and deliberately deformed by man, with its tortured, amputated limbs sticking out in all directions, demanding pity rather than praise. If you should happen to be reading these words during one of those long months in the year when the roses are not in bloom, push the book aside, walk out into the garden, and look at the poor things . . . really *look* at them, with an untarnished eye. What do you see? A long row of hospital cases. A collection of man-made shrubs which have served their purpose, and will not serve it again till their next brief period of flowering.

Over the years I have experimented with various devices in the hope of discovering some means by which hybrid teas can be harmonized with other flowers and shrubs. Thus, there was a season when I interplanted them with rue . . . the Jackman's Blue variety of *Ruta graveolens*. For a time they looked well enough, but during the summer the rue grew far too big, and did the roses no good. I could not help thinking, every time I passed them, how much better it would have been if instead of roses there had been lilies. The only time that roses were incorporated in the border with some degree of success was when we set three standard Étoile de Hollande immediately behind a bold clump of crimson pæonies. The flaunting leaves of the pæonies hid the gaunt stems of the roses, and when the two were in flower together there was an interesting floral argument between the two shades of red. But as soon as the pæonies died down the standards proclaimed themselves for the ugly things they were. The effect was rather as though somebody had absent-mindedly deposited an umbrella-stand in the middle of the border, so I gave them away to a lady who is an ardent supporter of the Rose Society. She was delighted and planted them at each corner of a triangular bed in the middle of the lawn, edged with blue lobelia. I understand that this design has given the greatest satisfaction.

This is about the sum total of my efforts to grow these roses in the garden. I remain convinced that it cannot be done, if we are aiming—as I hope we are—at natural perfection.

But when we come to climbing roses on the walls, that is a very different matter. So let us go outside, open the garden gate, step on to the Common, and see what we shall see.

When I came to live at Ham I was duly impressed by the thought that for the first time in my life I was residing in a cottage that was Crown Property, looking out on to land that was also Crown Property. I was not quite sure what this implied, because I am not very good at reading leases. There were a great many clauses about not knocking things down in the house or pulling things up in the garden, but these I interpreted generously; the Queen, surely, would not throw one into the Tower for uprooting fifty yards of diseased golden-rod, which was almost all I had to begin with. But there were also a number of rather sinister warnings—not in the lease but in correspondence with my solicitors— about 'abutting' and 'protruding' on to the Common, and these were more difficult to interpret. At a first reading these sounded as if tenants were being cautioned against sitting on the wall with their behinds hanging over the edge, and if I had been a fat lady in blue jeans I should have been the first to agree that such admonitions were salutary. But I was not a fat lady in blue jeans; I was a comparatively thin gentleman—or so I flattered myself—in grey flannel trousers.

This is where we can tell a story which will eventually lead us back to the roses. It begins with a crisis.

Where was I to find a place for my *Iris stylosa*? (To be *à la mode* we must now call them *Iris unguicularis* but I am growing too ancient to change the habits of a lifetime.) Crown Property the cottage might be, but without the sweet consolation of these flowers throughout the dark winter months, one would be sitting on an empty throne. There would be no more excited excursions over the snow-laden lawns to delve into the drifts and rescue them in bud, no more enchanted hours of watching them open in the firelight, no more echoes of dialogue with beloved—but faintly acidulous —friends. 'Yes, my dear, that's what you tell us, but I do really think that you're pulling the long bow a little bit, aren't you? I mean, these just can't have been picked this morning. It's about forty below zero and there's a howling gale and these are like orchids. Of course we all know that you've got the greenest of green fingers, but you see, I'm just a very ordinary sort of person, and I'm quite certain that they wouldn't do this for *me*.' After gallantly repudiating the suggestion that the lady is a very 'ordinary' sort of person—what an idea—one assures her that even if she were—though the very suggestion is ridiculous—the *Iris stylosa would* do it for her. And it would.

But where could I put them? These irises are not choosy, but if you are to grow them successfully you must meet their two basic demands. Firstly, you must plant them in a well-drained gritty soil—the sort of soil which nasturtiums would like. Secondly, you must give them a wall facing due south where they will get all the baking that our not very torrid climate can provide. The soil I could manage but the wall I could not.

Once again . . . where? All the time that I was asking this question I knew the answer, in my heart of hearts, but the answer was so shocking that I hardly dared to put it into words. The only place for the irises was *outside* the garden on the south wall facing the Common. This was in every way ideal. The soil was beautifully coarse and gritty, and whatever sunshine might come to us was soaked up by the old bricks and reflected back into the earth. But the soil was not my soil. It was the Crown's soil and it was also common property. And though, in my opinion, I should be embellishing the Crown with a great many exquisite jewels by planting it with *Iris stylosa*, I was a loyal citizen and I did not wish to do anything improper.

No, that is a howling lie. I wished to do something that was extremely improper.

So I began to make enquiries of my friends, with no great success, for they seemed to be even more apprehensive than myself.

B.N.　Do you know anything about abutting and protruding?

X.　　I beg your pardon?

B.N.　I mean legally. You see this is Crown Property and I want to plant something on the wall outside.

X.　　Oh my dear, I shouldn't do *that*.

B.N.　Why not?

X.　　Well, you know what Crown Property *is*?

B.N.　But that's precisely what I don't know.

X.　　The Crown goes quite mad if you so much as touch a *leaf*.

B.N.　But I only want to plant some irises. And I don't see why the Crown should ever find out.

X.　　It's probably got spies everywhere. For all you know we're being watched at this very moment.

B.N.　Do you think I might write to the Mayor?

X.　　My dear, that would be *fatal*.

B.N.　Why?

X.　　He's almost sure to be Labour. And he'd only say that you were a brutal capitalist encroaching on the living-spaces of the poor.

B.N. I don't think the Mayor's at all like that. Besides, I
       seem to remember that the Mayor's a woman.

X.   That only makes it worse. I really would *not* have any-
       thing to do with it unless you get one of the Royals to
       say you can. Do you think the Queen Mum could do
       something?

B.N. What could she do?

X.   Well, she adores flowers, and at least you've met her.

B.N. Only once, about forty years ago. And that's hardly
       an excuse for bothering her about a row of irises.

X.   You could say that it was for charity.

B.N. But it isn't.

X.   But you *do* open your garden for charity, and you
       could say that it helped to drag people in.

This is where at long last we return to the roses, as promised. For the plea of 'dragging people in' provided just the
sort of moral-legal excuse which was needed. True, it might
sound far-fetched in the depths of winter, if one were suddenly to be discovered by a park attendant, shovelling snow
away from the clumps. But it was worth the risk. So I went
ahead, and nobody said a thing, except that one of the aforesaid attendants said 'thank you', very sincerely, when I gave
him a glowing bouquet of the irises for his wife on Christmas
Eve.

The reason why the irises led to the roses was very simple,
and was based on the classic technique that was perfected by
Indian servants in the days of the British raj, when they
decided to purloin some valuable object, such as a cigarette
box, belonging to their employers. Instead of annexing the
box at one fell swoop they would move it, each day, nearer
and nearer to the door. If this passed unnoticed they would
then gently waft it into the hall, whence it drifted by slow

degrees towards the servants' quarters. During the war I used to watch these manoeuvres with the greatest fascination in my Bombay apartment and they undoubtedly influenced my conduct on Ham Common. For as soon as the irises were planted at the base of the wall it was obvious that the wall itself was crying out for roses and surely if I planted just one climber, nobody would notice? So I did, and nobody noticed. If one, why not two, and if two why not four? Finally, taking a deep breath, I ordered eight, choosing Golden Shower, which is one of the most valuable climbers ever perfected, of a clear banana yellow, exceptionally prolific, almost thornless and with a very long flowering period. You can see these roses, all through the summer, flaming like a beacon on the wall at the north end of the Common, and if any busybody were ever to complain I should fight him to the death.

I have nothing very new to say about climbing roses, apart from my original thesis that they are as much to be esteemed, for their musical qualities, as the hybrid teas are to be despised. There are seven in the garden. Here they are, with their appropriate composers:

Danse du Feu. This is Liszt, in the style of his Hungarian rhapsodies. With its scarlet cascades of blossom it has an almost excessive flamboyance—like Liszt himself in certain moods—so it is planted in semi-shade, climbing through the branches of one of the old pear trees.

Paul's Lemon Pillar. Pure Chopin. The flower of the nocturnes.

Mermaid. Although one is tempted to attribute this to Chopin I think that it is better given to Schubert, who might have written a song to it.

Albertine. I associate this with Lehar because it is the epitome of an old-fashioned operetta. It is so pink and fluffy and feminine that when you see it clambering round the bedroom windows you almost expect a rather elderly (but still attractive) soprano to pop her head through the curtains and burst into song. Stranger things have happened.

Guinee. This must go to Tschaikowski. It is the nearest to a black rose that I know of, and Tschaikowski wrote some very black music when he was in a mood of self-pity. There are many things to be said against Guinee. For example, it seems to attract an exceptional number of parasitic hangers-on. (So does Tschaikowski.) And the main stems of its branches have a habit of suddenly faltering and breaking off. (As with some of his melodies.) But at its best it is a great rose, as he is a great composer.

Cecile Brunner. I shall pin this, at random, in the buttonhole of Debussy. Although it is a 'China' rose it is very French. So was he. It is a tiny rose, with airy sprays of flesh-pink and —with no *arrière pensée*—he was also a tiny composer with airy sprays of flesh-pink. And it looks as though it had been born with the soft pedal on, which applies very much to Debussy. It is too painful to imagine what would happen to one's rendering of—say—'Jardins sous la Pluie', if anything went wrong with the soft pedal.

Violette. A bunch of these little roses would look charming on a harpsichord, which is why I shall present it to Couperin. It is very aptly named, for the flowers recall very dark double violets. And if, like myself, you have no space for the 'old' roses, it makes a very good substitute.

That is the sum total of my climbing roses, and the composers who accompany them. I would like to have some Bach roses but as far as I am aware—the reader is at liberty to contradict me, for the floor is wide open to debate—there are none. If we had to choose a flower for Bach it would probably be the Madonna Lily. But neither he nor Beethoven really brings flowers to mind; they are trees, giants of the forest; indeed, they are forests in themselves, surging and straining in immortal winds of music. Whereas Mozart is full of flowers, and especially roses—the wild roses of the hedgerow.

It occurs to me that among the readers who have been grappling with the last few pages there may be some who, through no fault of their own, are tone-deaf. They must have been having a very bad time. It is too late to do anything about it, for I really cannot be expected to cross out hundreds of words on a subject about which I feel so strongly, but I can perhaps make amends by telling them a story. A nice story always brightens up the page. And though this one has a musical theme it also introduces a nice animal, which brightens up the page even more. The animal is—or, alas, was—my own cat Five, who passed from this world last Christmas Eve. This was for me a day of great mourning, but at least I could console myself with the thought that his life had been long and happy, and that he went on his way with ease and dignity. For he was twenty-one years old, and he died with a purr in his throat, and he had finished his last saucer of milk.

Five was an extraordinary cat—though all cats, of course, are extraordinary—and if any of our scruffy young drama-tists had any sense they would write a play about him. The predominating theme of modern drama may be loosely described as 'lack of communication'. An actor enters from the left, an actress enters from the right, a third character (usually a tramp) enters up stage centre, and for the next three hours they proceed to say things to one another which they understand very little and the audience understands not at all. Five would not have stood that sort of nonsense. He knew very well how to 'communicate'; he made it known, in no uncertain terms, when he wished to eat, to sleep, to be lifted up, to be set down; he had an exceptionally wide feline vocabulary and was a past-master in the art of the 'hich'—that alarming noise, as of escaping gas, which is employed by cats in moments of indignation. But most of all he liked to be communicated *to*; he liked to listen to conversation, and in particular, to music. Which is why I shall here recount the following story.

Ce soir on était ravi

Five and the Nightingales

I have always believed that between animals and music there exists a strange affinity. The cobra coils to the lilt of the flute, the circus bear dances to the cruel rhythm of the drum, and I once had a long and intimate association with a thrush who used to accompany me outside the window of the music-room while I was wrestling—shadow-boxing would be a more accurate way of describing it—with the misty and intricate harmonies of Granados's 'Maiden and the Nightingale'.

'All art,' wrote Walter Pater, 'constantly aspires towards the condition of music.' So, I believe, does all Nature. For those who have ears to hear, all the winds are laden with melody; and whatever the wild waves may be saying, they are making music, beautiful music—the surging music of spray and rhythmic water, against the dark staves of the rocks, through the shifting sharps and trebles of the sands.

Five was one of the many small creatures who seemed to hear this natural music and to rejoice in it.

When we first came to the cottage I could not understand why Five, as the evenings of spring began to lengthen across the lawn, showed so many signs of restlessness and tension. True, during these early weeks we thought it wiser to keep him indoors at night, for he is so plump and pretty that he puts wrong ideas into the heads of the local toms. Much to his own astonishment, for there has never been any reason to suppose that he has any abnormal psychological tendencies.

Usually Five is happy to go to bed early; he is not of a specially nocturnal disposition. But now, he began to act out of character, and whenever I took him into Gaskin's room to curl him up on his favourite chair, there were protests. There were scratchings on the door, leapings on to the window-ledge, and tail-twitchings. One evening, observing these antics and trying to interpret them, I suddenly realized what was the matter. From the distance came the faint sound of nightingales. Five had heard them and his hunting instincts—so I foolishly imagined—had been aroused. If there had been the smallest chance that he might catch one of them I need hardly say that he would have been put firmly back to bed. However, such a prospect was academic;

164

even in his early youth Five had caught nothing save an occasional worm or a very sleepy bumblebee. So I opened the window and let him go.

Then I walked out to see what was happening. In a very few moments I saw that I had done Five a grave injustice in supposing him to be moved by the instincts of the hunter. He had loftier motives. He was a music-lover, and he wished to listen to the concert.

There could be no doubt about it. The nightingales were singing at the end of the lawn, one in the apple tree and one in the old pear, like two *prima donnas* performing from rival stages. If Five had been animated by even the smallest trace of malice he would have been prowling about in the shadows, or crouching concealed in a bush, waiting to pounce. But no; he was sitting quite still, with his back to me, sharply illuminated by the moon, in a state of total ecstasy.

Unfortunately, the advent of so appreciative an audience, who had obviously paid for his seat, was misinterpreted by the nightingales. Or maybe fortunately, for their performance now took an extra, acid brilliance; golden thunderbolts of melody were hurled against Five, and if cadenzas could kill he would have been pierced to the heart. But he, in his turn, misinterpreted the nightingales, and the only result of this quickening of the tempo, this extra sparkle in the coloratura passages, was to increase his enchantment. Five rose, his plump body swaying ever so slightly, as though he were intoxicated by the beauty of it all, and staggered to the trunk of the pear in order to be nearer to the stage. There was a quick change in the ornithological dispositions, and the pear-tree nightingale shot across to the golden acacia, where it proceeded to produce such a shower of hostile trills and cadenzas that Five, if he had only known what it was all about, would have fled in dismay. But Five had no idea what it was all about; to him, this was a concert given for his especial benefit. 'More . . . more!' he seemed to be pleading as he gazed at the stars, and after an especially accomplished passage, which would have tied the average *diva* into knots, he was so *exalté* that he reeled over to the trunk of the willow and started scratching it in sheer abandon. This was too much for the nightingales. Each of them emitted an outraged high C; there was a swirl of wings and a swift shadow across the moon; the concert was over.

Five stayed there for a while. Then he stalked slowly homewards across the lawn, down the little path that leads to Gaskin's back-yard, and pushed his way through the cat door. I was reminded of an elderly gentleman thrusting through the velvet curtains of an alcove in the Comédie Française, still dazed by the beauty of a ballet-dancer. '*Ce soir*,' he murmured, '*on était ravi*.' Five does not speak French. But when I stroked him, as he sank exhausted into his chair, sparks crackled from his tail.

CHAPTER ELEVEN

THE FELINE TOUCH

A GARDEN without cats, it will be generally agreed, can scarcely deserve to be called a garden at all. There is something dead about a lawn which has never been shadowed by the swift silhouette of a dancing kitten, and much of the magic of the heather beds would vanish if, as we bent over them, there was no chance that we might hear a faint rustle among the blossoms, and find ourselves staring into a pair of sleepy, green eyes.

Lest the reader should complain that we are straying too far from the realms of horticulture I would reply that the cats have had—quite literally—a considerable influence in the actual shape that the garden has taken. I should always have given prominence to these heather beds but I doubt whether they would have spread so far across the lawns if it had not been for the fact that they formed so perfect a setting for the feline arts which we are about to describe. Which brings us to the story of

The Ballets of Anthony and Trollop

Descriptions of other people's cats, as far as their purely physical appearance is concerned, are almost as boring as descriptions of other people's babies. A large portion of my life is spent in reading accounts of the smudges on the noses or the kinks in the tails of felines residing in all parts of the Commonwealth, and though I should doubtless approve of the smudges and respond to the kinks if I were to meet the owners, I cannot raise a purr out of them on paper. So we will merely inform the reader that Anthony and Trollop, the two presiding geniuses of my household, are half-caste Siamese, black as your hat, with eyes like moonstones. In spite of a staggering capacity for fish they are as slim as straws and so swift and elegant that they would make a professional model look as if she were wearing hob-nail boots.

So much for their outward guise; more would be tedious. When we come to their souls it is a different matter, for the souls of some cats, I suspect, may be more worthy of exploration than the souls of some humans. Since this is a strictly practical volume, we will content ourselves by observing that they have the souls of artists, and a quite exceptional appreciation of the beauties of Nature.

However, it was some weeks before these qualities were to be made manifest.

When Anthony and Trollop first took up residence at the

cottage their sole knowledge of Nature had been confined to what could be seen through the narrow window of a bed-sitting-room in the Queen's Road. This was not much. True, as their small noses pressed against the glass, they may have noted the shapes and shadows of the clouds above the roofs, and as they curled forlornly on the counterpane, gaining comfort from the shelter of each other's arms, their sharp black pointed ears may have heard the patter of the rain and the sighing of the wind in the grey, cavernous streets outside their prison cell. There may even have been times when they gazed, in wild surmise, at the sudden apparition of a London sparrow, alighting casually on the window-ledge, and cocking a snoop at them with a cheeky flutter before it swooped away. What such a vision must have done to them, what strange torturing emotions it must have evoked, what distant jungle music it must have sent drumming through their brains . . . only the pen of a great poet could describe it, and, even then, he would have to mix his ink with tears. There is great majesty, and undying awe, in the spectre of Blake's burning tiger. But there is the sum of all pathos and the scope for all pity in the picture of two small creatures hunched together at the window of a London flat.

So when Anthony and Trollop arrived, and for the first time were carried into the garden, one at a time, held very tightly lest they should take a leap into the unknown, they were ill-equipped to cope with the alarms and enigmas of Nature in the raw. They had never seen a blade of grass. Their fur had never been caressed by the invisible fingers of the wind. The rustle of leaves was as strange to them as the music of the birds, and their noses were assailed by a thousand unfamiliar scents. They were as lost and shrinking and bewildered as any of ourselves might be if, for the first time, we stepped from a space capsule into the valleys of the moon.

Needless to say, we proceeded very gradually, step by step. I would get a firm grip on Anthony while Gaskin held Trollop by the window in order that he might be a spectator of what was going on. Then I would open the door of the porch, very gently, and step outside. This was an immediate signal for frenzied struggles with all four feet at once, but these would slowly quieten down. And then I would hear the little heart thumping at an alarming pace, while the small black nostrils sniffed in the exciting elixirs borne on the wind. A few more steps, and we were in the shadow of the pear tree, with a green branch trembling only a few feet away. Now I would whisper words of reassurance. 'You see, Anthony, it is quite all right. This is a tree, and it is a friend. This is a tree that soon you will be climbing. Just a tree.' And then, when the tree had been—as it were—'accepted' I would kneel down and take a paw and draw it gently over the grass. 'And this, Anthony, is grass. Feel how soft it is. The grass is a friend too, and soon you will be running over it, and if ever you feel upset you will wish to nibble it and it will make you better.' By now, as likely as not, the shock of these revelations would have caused Anthony's legs to struggle once again, telling me that he had taken all that he was capable of standing. Whereupon we would beat a hasty retreat to the porch, close the door, release Anthony, and go over to repeat the entire process with Trollop.

In a moment we shall be describing the choreographic inception of the first ballet, and I must apologize for these preliminaries to all those balletomanes who are doubtless awaiting with impatience a revelation of such importance. But in order that the credits for the creation of the opus may be allotted with absolute authority, so that there may be no

critical controversy in years to come, I must here explain
that the ballet was only made possible by the widely diverg-
ent personalities of its two exponents. Anthony and Trollop,
in spite of their physical resemblance, are temperamentally
miles apart. For some weeks after their arrival I was only
able to identify them by a small white spot on the fur in the
neighbourhood of Trollop's behind, so that if there was ever
any argument—if, for example, we were at a loss to decide
which of them had just devoured two plates of fish—we were
obliged to turn them upside down and gaze, with suitable
diffidence, at their posteriors. However, as time went on
their personalities began to proclaim themselves, and these
personalities, by a happy chance, were aptly reflected in
their names. Anthony began to reveal many saintly qualities;
he would sit for hours in profound meditation, gazing at the
clouds while Trollop . . . well, Trollop really was a trollop.
If you met him walking down the garden path, he would
pause, cock his head, and then fall flat on his back, display-
ing his white spot with shameless abandon, and demand
tummy-rubbings. When you bent down to pick him up it
was like putting a nearly-boiling kettle on the gas-ring; he
burst instantly into a purr of such full-throated ecstasy that
one feared that he would choke. And indeed, he frequently
did . . . so that his purr, if one were to interpret it musically,
would be an alternation of woodwind trills and faint per-
cussions. Purr . . . gulp . . . purr . . . gulp. Whereas Anthony,
before he purrs, must be wooed, very gently, until one hears
a sort of muted organ music starting up inside him—a music
which slowly swells to a chorale in praise of the whole
feline world.

From these two personalities, Anthony the introvert and

Trollop the extrovert, the first ballet—the famous 'Erica'—was created, and though the student may find this difficult to believe, the basic outlines of the work had been fixed within only ten days of the kittens' arrival.

It happened like this. In our trips round the garden, Trollop proved by far the more adventurous. He could soon be set down on the grass without any danger of his shooting off, terrified, into outer space (Ham Common). True, the vast areas of the lawn, which must have appeared to him much as the open Atlantic appeared to Columbus, were obviously intimidating, and during his first journeys he hugged the shore, keeping within the friendly shelter of the shrubs. But on the third morning he decided to take the plunge. He emerged from beneath a philadelphus, and set out for the unknown, occasionally glancing over his shoulder, prowling very slowly, with his small paws pushed forward one after the other, as though he were a swimmer doing a breast-stroke. Half-way across there came a lunatic cackle from a blackbird, who had been watching the proceedings with evident distaste from the branches of the pear tree. This proved too much for his brave little heart and he leapt forward, as one demented, with no idea of where he was heading. Fortunately for him (and for the future of ballet in general), he made straight for the broad, friendly bank of the heather, and once he was inside it he was so enraptured by this strange new world, with its branches towering over his head, its deep purple shadows, and the ghostly chime of a thousand flower bells, that he began to bounce about in it, and even, after a few minutes, to make a tentative pounce at an outraged bumblebee. From that moment onwards Trollop had the freedom of the garden, but for some time he continued to use the heather bed as though it were a sort of base camp, making straight for it, pausing to get his bearings, and then setting out on his explorations, north, south, east and west, in ever widening circles.

Would Anthony find in the heather bed the same assurance and the same inspiration? Although he was still in the arm-carrying stage, I decided to put the question to the test. One morning—a quiet, golden morning, with no disturbing orchestrations in the music of the copper-beech—I carried him across the infinite spaces of the lawn, deposited him firmly in the centre of a large clump of *Erica vagans*, and retreated to await developments. And that was really when the ballet was born. For Trollop, the bold one, happened at that very moment to be returning to base after an exceptionally daring exploration, and when he saw the top of Anthony's tail emerging from the heather something must have stirred in his heart—some prowling, primitive jungle rhythm which caused him to dash forward and, with a single breathtaking *entrechat* in the true Russian tradition, precipitate himself upon Anthony's tail. Whereupon Anthony, partly no doubt from sheer terror, but also, I believe, in response to the innate sense of drama which makes all cats the masters of any stage they may be called upon to tread, leapt even higher. And for several minutes I was the solitary, enraptured onlooker at one of the most spectacular choreographic improvisations that the world can ever have known. Nureyev, confronted by an exercise of such virtuosity, would have hung his head in shame. Up leapt Anthony, up leapt Trollop, tails lashing in rhythms of indescribable grace, legs performing exercises which would have taxed the technical resources of a Nijinski. The lithe black bodies glistened in the sunlight like ebony butterflies, seeming to hang suspended in the air; and then, of a sudden, they disappeared again

173

into the enveloping curtains of the heather, and there was stillness, and an almost unbearable tension. The many distinguished persons who have been privileged to witness *Ballet Erica* in its repeat performance have all agreed that it is this instantaneous transition from violent action to total stillness that gives the ballet its unique quality, and entitles it to a permanent place among the world's classics.

Footnote for the historian. After this immense burst of creative effort both kittens were in a state of nervous exhaustion for twenty-four hours. But at dusk on the following evening they repaired once again to the heather bed, and worked with great energy at the basic outlines of the opus, which today remains, by and large, as bold and flowing as at the moment of its conception.

Ballet de l'Escalier

I venture to claim some credit for this work, which has proved among the most popular in the repertoire. One morning, walking across the garden with a pair of steps, I was called to the telephone. Hurrying to answer the call, I left the steps in the middle of the lawn, and on returning discovered that Trollop was sitting on top of them. Here was a situation of great dramatic promise, made all the more striking by the stark simplicity of the décor . . . the empty stage of the lawn, the dark curtains of the copper-beech, and in the centre, the solitary 'prop' of the steps, surmounted by the slim black figure of Trollop, who looked as though he was clad, from top to toe, in black skin tights. One was reminded of the ballet drawings of Degas. The only doubt was . . . would the kittens appreciate the golden opportunity with which chance had presented them?

I need not have asked so foolish a question. No sooner was

174

Anthony fetched from the house and set on the edge of the lawn, in sight of the steps, than he caught the idea and fell —as it were—'into rhythm', stalking slowly across the lawn towards his partner who, without a moment's hesitation, leaned backwards with a gesture of indescribable grace, waiting for the *pas de deux* to begin. I will not take up the reader's time in describing this long and intricate dance, which makes more strenuous demands on the performers than any of the duets in Swan Lake. However—again for the benefit of the historian—I may mention one fascinating variation of it to which I, so far, have been the sole witness.

The importance of this variation is due to the fact it was the means of recalling from retirement no less a star than Five, whose dancing days, so we all imagined, were long passed.

When the kittens arrived at the cottage Five—a very sedate and distinguished tabby of pronounced *embonpoint*— greeted them with suitable hauteur, and though there was no actual physical combat, there were alarming oral encounters, growls and sounds of escaping gas, and haughty exits through the cat door. However, it soon became evident that although Five was no longer physically equipped to play the roles in which he might have dazzled us in days gone by, the glamour of the stage still held him. He was passionately interested in all that was going on. Whenever the pair of steps was placed in the centre of the lawn, as a signal that a performance of the ballet was about to be given, he would take up his place at the window, and sit with his nose pressed close to the glass, waiting with ill-concealed impatience for the rise of the curtain. He was like an elderly *première danseuse* in a box at the opera, preparing to pass judgement on a rising star who was about to re-enact some

G

role in which she herself had triumphed. And pass judgement Five most certainly did. If the dancing was not quite up to standard, if Trollop missed his footing on the steps, or if Anthony suddenly acted out of character by deciding to chase a bee, there would be disdainful sniffs from Five, and temperamental tail-lashings, and even, on occasions, a swift and contemptuous exit from the box, or rather, from the window-ledge.

And then there came a day when Five could no longer endure the role of passive spectator. For some reason or other the kittens were giving a very slipshod performance. Trollop so far forgot himself as to leap off the steps and start chasing his own tail, while Anthony—this was quite inexcusable—interrupted an important solo passage in order to go off-stage and powder his nose in the herbaceous border. If a feline Diaghileff had been sitting in the stalls, sparks would have flown.

So Five, who had been trained in the strictest classical traditions, decided to shame them. Like an outsize Ulanova leaping from the wings he bounced off the window ledge, shook himself, and stalked out through the porch. So great was the force of his personality that as he stepped somewhat heavily on to the grass the kittens were aware of his presence; Trollop stopped chasing his tail and Anthony, his nose-powdering forgotten, stayed stock-still, in a frozen position, with one paw curved above the earth. Five cast them a single chilling glance and then—aware that he had the audience in his grip—proceeded towards the centre of the stage with the total assurance of a professional, dedicated artist. If I were to say that what followed was the greatest choreographic display of all time, I should be exaggerating. With so rotund and substantial a body, such a feat would obviously be impossible. But the technique—the glorious classical technique —was there. At the bottom of the steps he *sketched* an *entre-chat*, and though the plump legs were not quite capable of sustaining the weight of his fall, the movement had a most touching grace. And though, in his wisdom, he did not ascend to the top of the steps, he *sketched* the flight that he might have made, in those far-off days, and stayed there with one paw lifted, and his green eyes staring to the sky. And then, in a plump, furry abandon, he cavorted round the base of the steps, pointing his paws, and waving his tail, and for a few magical moments I saw again the Five that I had loved and applauded so long ago, a whole seventeen years ago, which in the life of a cat is nearing a century. Even his pauses, which the cynic might have attributed to a shortage of breath, had a sort of classical authority, and after the last pause he slowly walked off the stage into the wings, holding his tail very high, and giving it an occasional flick, as though to acknowledge the plaudits of Anthony and Trollop who— to their credit—had followed the whole performance with breathless interest, realizing, as they must have done, that for a few fleeting moments they had been in the presence of a Master.

Feuilles D'Automne

This charming trifle is a special favourite of mine, so much so that on some golden afternoons in October, when there is still enough warmth in the sunshine for the windows of the music room to be opened, I have amused myself by accompanying it on the piano, improvising in the manner —at least I like to think that it is the manner—of such minor composers as Chaminade and Delibes. The title explains itself. The strict purist may object that it is too loose and fluid in form to rate as a classic, and we must admit that it relies, to a very large extent, on the improvisation of the moment. How could it be otherwise when the whole nature of the choreography is dictated by the fickle fancies of the wind? If there are strong gusts from the south-west, which strip the leaves from the copper-beech with restless masculine fingers, the whole tempo of the ballet is set to *allegro con brio*, and the stage of the lawn is greatly extended, in order that the kittens may have the fullest scope in their leaf-chasing, for such variations as may occur to them. But if the airs are tranquil, so that the dark leaves flutter down one by one, falling to the grass with a gentle sigh, the tempo slows down; and though the dramatic tension is in no way decreased, the actual *line* of the ballet is predominantly *legato*, with slow, sinuous prowlings from the shadows, ending in a single brilliant *entrechat*, as one of the kittens, its black fur glistening in the sunshine, pounces on a leaf and, in a simulated frenzy of desire, proceeds to demolish it.

By the time that these words are published there is every hope, as we suggested above, that several other ballets will have been sketched out and put into active rehearsal. Indeed, an entire new series is at this moment under contemplation, inspired by the flood-lighting lamp which on summer evenings creates patterns of almost melodramatic beauty among the dark recesses of the copper-beech. This ballet may well mark a turning-point in the whole history of the art, if only because it commands the services of a highly accomplished chorus, free of charge, in the shape of the moths who flutter around in the brilliant lights. These creatures, as is to be expected, inspire the kittens to perform feats of exceptional virtuosity.

Some readers, whose feline propensities are comparatively undeveloped, may feel that in a small garden such ballets as we have been describing might prove impractical, or even dangerous. It would be a great pity if they were to retain this illusion, for by discouraging their cats from this form of self-expression they might, however inadvertently, be robbing the world of some choreographic masterpiece.

The harm done by cats is negligible. Naturally, if a gardener is so foolish as to leave seed-boxes all over the place, he is asking for trouble; cats have been brought up by humans to regard these utensils as powdering closets, and as such they promptly use them. To fail to do so, they doubtless imagine, would be discourteous. And if the gardener leaves a window of the greenhouse ajar, and if a cat, making its tour of inspection, observes a patch of sunlight falling across a row of pots, the cat can hardly be blamed for jumping in, and curling up among the pots to bask in the warm glow that pervades them. He may—though rarely—knock one over; but the sheer delight of finding a cat in a greenhouse at all is more than adequate compensation for so trifling a mishap. What combination of circumstances could be more charming, more spiritually therapeutic? One opens the door and breathes in the scent of the leaves and the petals—the bittersweet tang of the geraniums and the moss-like fragrance of the hanging ferns—and then one suddenly observes a small black bundle, stretched across the skirting in an attitude of total abandon, with the petal of a begonia stuck to the end of its tail. The paws are lazily thrown back in a gesture of allurement, and as one bends down, a green eye opens and a tail twitches, very slightly, acknowledging one's caresses but also indicating that for the moment they are not essential.

CHAPTER TWELVE

A QUESTION OF DESIGN

WHENEVER the garden is open to the public it is
fairly certain that before the afternoon is over
some lady will approach with furtive suggestions
that she should be led to a quiet corner in order to discuss a
matter of confidence. In the early days, I assumed that these
ladies wished to powder their noses, and conducted them to
the appropriate offices. However this led to puzzling situa-
tions, for they had no desire to powder their noses; they were
after something very different. They wanted me to design
their gardens for them, on what is known as 'a business basis',
and they were at a loss to understand why such transactions
should be conducted in the loo.

To be asked to design other people's gardens is flattering, particularly when the people who seek advice have understood what one has been trying to do in one's own garden and have appreciated one's basic principles—the elimination of squares and triangles, the flow of melodic lines, the vital part played by water, the many *trompe l'oeil* devices which double the area, the use of colour, and especially of coloured foliage. And I can imagine no more pleasing profession than that of the landscape gardener—always providing that one's employer was a millionaire of a docile temperament, who would guarantee to leave the country for at least three years while one was getting on with the job, and would give an undertaking, on his return, to refrain from changing the disposition of a single leaf. In these days such patrons are few and far between, so that one wonders whether the landscape gardener has much of a future. However, it is his present that here concerns me, the trials and tribulations of his job as he goes about his daily business. These I can best describe by an account of my own experiences, on the few occasions when I have tried to help people 'on a business basis'.

We will call the first lady Mrs Lewis. She was a blonde of about thirty-five, with a buxom figure, a turned-up nose, and immense blue eyes, which regarded the world with evident complacency. She inhabited a large neo-Tudor house some ten miles west of London, whither I was bidden to tea. Her husband, who was not at home, was 'something in the city' —a very affluent something, judging by the Italian Primitives in the hall. In spite of the fact that she had apparently just emerged from a bath of Lanvin's Arpège, and omitted to dry herself, she was rather nice. She was certainly all eagerness to make a garden. Tea had scarcely been served, with a great clatter of neo-Georgian silver, before she had sprung to her feet and was conducting me to the terrace.

'If only,' she cried, 'if only you could make me something beautiful out of this!'

Before us stretched a bleak square of about two acres, entirely surrounded by a new brick wall about eight feet high. Behind this wall, at irregular intervals, loomed the roofs of her neighbours' houses, which were comparatively small, and clustered around like poor relations. The main feature of the 'garden' was a rockery of singular repulsiveness, jutting out from a geometrical complex of triangular rose beds. (I suspected, rightly, that she had designed it herself.) In the distance was a tennis court entirely surrounded, on all four sides, by asparagus beds.

'Well,' I said, with feigned brightness, 'we can but try.'

'And where do I begin?' she demanded. 'That is what baffles me. What must I do to *begin* with?'

The answer to this question was simple, but difficult to phrase politely. What Mrs Lewis must do to begin with was to go away, immediately, and as far as possible. It is quite impossible to design anything of any value with people breathing down one's neck. One needs total solitude to arrange even a bunch of flowers.

But how to explain this to Mrs Lewis?

'In your book,' she said, 'you wrote that you always began with water. Now, where shall we put our water?'

'That depends on what sort of water you want—whether it's merely to be part of the design—just a patch of silver—or whether you want to grow things in it. Lilies, for instance.'

'I must have masses and *masses* of lilies!'

183

'In that case . . .'

But she was not listening. 'I thought . . . over there. By the wall.'

Her hand swept to the right, to a patch of lawn that was in deep shade.

'I'm afraid that wouldn't do.'

'Not *do*? Why?'

'Because if you want water-lilies they must be in full sunlight.'

'*All* water-lilies?'

'All that will grow in this country.'

'Are you sure?'

'Quite sure.'

'Well, of course, if you say so.' She frowned. 'Then what do you suggest?'

'I would make a circular pool bang in the middle of the lawn and just see what happens. As soon as it's in being, it'll start to suggest things.' I pointed ahead to a distance of about thirty yards. 'Out there, for instance, where you've put the deck chairs and the parasols.'

'That would be *quite* impossible.'

'Why?'

'Because that's where Mr Lewis likes to do his sunbathing.'

'But couldn't he sunbathe by the lily-pool?'

'I don't think he'd care for it,' she observed. 'I don't think you know Mr Lewis.'

She was well aware that I did not know Mr Lewis.

'If there's a mosquito within a hundred miles,' she continued, 'it goes straight for Mr Lewis. So we'll have to think of somewhere else, shan't we?'

'There doesn't seem to be anywhere else—except the tennis court.'

'You're not suggesting that we should put the pool in the tennis court?'

'No. But we might do away with the tennis court altogether.'

'Do *away* with it? But it's only just been put in!'

'Then couldn't we screen it off?'

'How?'

'Well . . . we could plant groups of conifers round it. And we could mask all that ugly wire-netting with climbing roses, and honeysuckles, and that sort of thing.'

She shook her head energetically. 'I doubt whether that would appeal to Mr Lewis. In fact, I'm sure it wouldn't. You see, he takes his tennis very seriously. He's having lessons from a professional. And somehow . . . roses and honeysuckles . . . and *professional* tennis . . . they don't seem to go together.'

'Perhaps not. All the same, if you really want a lily-pool . . .'

'I can't *live* without a lily-pool!'

I scanned the horizon. In the furthest corner there was an old curved wall that looked as though it might be concealing some little secret garden. One might contrive something quite pleasing there, provided that there was enough sunlight. It wouldn't be ideal but it would be better than nothing.

So I said to Mrs Lewis, 'What goes on behind that wall?'

'Nothing. Just a lot of rubbish heaps. Why?'

'Couldn't we put the water garden in *there*? And add to the height of the wall, and make a rather pretty path—in old red brick—leading up to it?' For the first time in this frustrating conversation, I began to feel a spark of enthusiasm. 'We might find a pair of old Italian gates, in wrought iron. And we could have a fountain. And the whole thing could be self-contained, with a lovely element of surprise. And if you take my advice, you'd keep everything pure white. Lilies, white foxgloves, white roses, clusters of white phlox, hostas with white-and-green leaves . . .'

And then I caught her eye. She was staring at me with the sort of expression that a nurse in a mental hospital might reserve for a patient who, though not violent, was exceptionally tiresome.

She spoke slowly and very clearly, with a great deal of lip movement, as though addressing a deaf-mute. 'Mr Nichols, I don't think you quite understand the situation. You see, I have two small children.' She paused and then added— her lips working overtime—'Very Small Children.'

She made them sound like midgets.

'Yes?'

'I *have* to think of them.'

I felt like saying, 'So what?' If you are a millionairess, equipped with midgets, you probably think of very little else.

'Of course.'

'You understand?'

I did not understand at all. 'I'm afraid . . .'

She interrupted me with a tinkling laugh. 'It's easy to see you're a bachelor!' She was still very friendly. She laid a gentle hand on my arm. 'If *you* had two Very Small Children, would you like to think of them Out There'—she pointed, as though to immense distances—'out of sight, out of sound?'

At last I thought I understood. 'I don't think they'd do much harm.'

'*Do* much harm?' She removed her hand abruptly. 'But what about *them*?'

'Oh, I see. You mean, they might fall in?'

'That is precisely what I mean.'

186

'But that wouldn't matter at all,' I said brightly. 'The water need be only eighteen inches deep.' Since she made no comment I continued. 'In fact, there are several lilies which do quite well in only fifteen inches. Of course, you'd have to top the pool up in the summer but I imagine that would present no problems?'

She achieved a smile, with a great effort. 'I'm afraid,' she said, 'we seem to be talking a different language. I mean—the very idea—I should never have a moment's peace.' Another heroic smile. 'Well, that would seem to be the end of our little pool, wouldn't it?'

I made a last effort. 'Have you thought of the entrance?'

'What about the entrance?'

'Well, you have a very large courtyard. If it were treated formally . . .'

She shook her head with great emphasis. 'That would be *out* of the question. The cars!'

'What cars?'

'Mr Lewis has three cars, in *constant* use. He *has* to.'

'But I thought I saw two quite substantial garages?'

She ignored the interruption. 'Apart from that he does a great deal of entertaining. He *has* to.'

'But couldn't his guests park in the road?'

Her only answer was a pitying smile.

Out of politeness, she asked me to stay for another half-hour, and conducted me round the rest of the garden. And out of politeness I continued to make suggestions, knowing full well that they would all be flatly rejected. Remove two of the asparagus beds? Impossible! If there was one thing that Mr Lewis really doted on, it was his asparagus. Block out the surrounding houses with screens of conifers? But they would take so long to grow, and it would hardly be neighbourly, would it? Mr Lewis was held in great esteem by the neighbours. Modify the rockery? What did I mean by 'modify'? What I meant, of course, was throw the whole horrid thing on to the rubbish heap, but I could hardly say that, since Mrs Lewis informed me that she had designed it herself.

So after a decent interval I looked at my watch, remarked upon the lateness of the hour, and suggested that perhaps the best plan would be for me to make a rough sketch-map to send to her for her approval—an idea which she accepted with relief, as likely to get us both out of a somewhat embarrassing situation.

On the way out I met Mr Lewis letting himself into the hall. He was quite different from what I had expected. He appeared to be younger than his wife and he looked more like a country squire than a city man. After offering me a drink, which I declined, he turned to Mrs Lewis.

'Well, darling, everything settled?'

She smiled wanly. 'One can't make a garden overnight, dear. As Mr Nichols would be the first to tell you.'

'Of course not. All the same, I bet that we shan't be long, once you get cracking.' He winked at me. 'Wonderful woman, my wife. Knows what she wants and usually gets it.'

'All the same'—I could not resist the temptation to say this—'I gather that you have some fairly strong views yourself? About the garden, I mean?'

'Me? Good Lord, no! Leave it entirely to her. If she wants to flood the whole damned thing and turn it into a lake, God bless her! *I* shan't complain. By the way, *is* that what she wants to do?'

'I'm not quite sure.' My eyes met those of Mrs Lewis.

188

'There's still a great deal to be discussed. And please don't bother . . . I can see myself out.'

So much for Mrs Lewis. Because I liked her, in spite of her silliness, I sent her the sketch-map. Which she acknowledged, with a very nice letter, and a large jar of caviar, the most expensive variety obtainable, and all the more delicious for being free of tax. That represents just about the sum total of the rewards I have received in the profession of landscape gardening.

The episode of Mrs Lewis—minus the caviar—is typical of each and every occasion on which I have been rash enough to give advice 'on a business basis'. I have come to the conclusion that Mrs Lewis must be a universal figure.

There was for instance, an incredibly rich woman in, let us say, Hampshire, who resided in an enormous house near the sea, entirely surrounded by roses. If you had surveyed the estate from a helicopter you would have been justified in assuming that you were passing over a rose nursery, particularly as they were all arranged in square beds. Having visited my own garden, and having swooned in the usual manner, she invited me to stay for the week-end, and since the party included several charming friends, I was very happy to go. It was all most enjoyable, as a social interlude, but as a professional exercise it was a complete flop. When I suggested that she was 'over-rosed' she stared at me with incredulity. How *could* one be 'over-rosed'? I must be joking. 'It was *impossible* to have too many roses.' She stated this as a fundamental law of nature. But no, I said, it was possible to have a great deal too many roses, and she had them. And since she also had eight gardeners, and a wonderful soil, and a lovely lie of the land, with gentle slopes leading down to a lake, it seemed a great pity that all she had done with it was to plant it in solid blocks of red and white and pink and yellow. Even the old grey walls, which cried aloud for magnolias, were smothered in roses. If I were going to have any say in the matter at all, I must be allowed to plough up at least four acres of rose-beds and begin all over again. But I might have been speaking to the deaf, and although the week-end passed with great amiability, the subject of gardening was no more mentioned.

It seems a pity because—well, one has ideas, and I think that they are good ones. Sometimes I have said to myself, 'Oh for an hour of Capability Brown! At least he would have understood what one was trying to say.' But if Capability Brown had lived in our times I doubt whether he would have found the sort of patrons who used to support him. The days have long vanished when the artist could look the patron in the eye and tell him precisely what he proposed to do and how he proposed to do it. And then—most important of all—tell the patron to *go away*.

However, there have been a few happy exceptions. Once, in the South of France, an eccentric millionaire asked me what should be done about his cliffs. I told him, and he actually did it, with sensational results. They were vast, jagged cliffs, stretching dramatically to the sea, plentifully pock-marked with little natural saucers of coarse red earth. At random I suggested that he should create a floral Niagara of nasturtiums, in every conceivable shade of scarlet and orange and lemon yellow and cinnamon. To my astonishment, instead of changing the subject, he called for his secretary and told her to get on the telephone and buy nasturtium seeds in staggering quantities, from Paris,

London and New York. A few days later they began to arrive by the sack and a very enjoyable, though somewhat vertiginous, time was had by all, as we clambered about the cliffs, clinging to stumps of broom and gorse, high above the peacock-blue waters of the Mediterranean, scattering nasturtium seeds in all directions. Later that summer I went down again. He met me at the airport, in a state of some excitement, and instead of going home to the villa we drove to Villefranche harbour, boarded the yacht, and sailed round the cape till we were opposite his estate. And there they were, the nasturtiums, foaming down the cliffs in a cascade of colour, a Niagara of blossom, blazing away in the sunshine so brilliantly that they were still visible far out to sea.

But that was nearly twenty years ago; and the flowers must long since have been shrivelled by the hot summer or washed from their precarious pockets by the winter rains. I have not been to look. For my friend is dead, and I suspect that I shall not meet his like again.

As I said before, it seems a pity. There are so many things that might be done, if only the people who had the money would use a little imagination or take a little advice. Admittedly, most of the money is now at the disposal of the State, but why should we not have a Ministry of Gardens? For the cost of a single atom bomb—or whatever other form of malevolent idiocy we may be investing in by the time these words are printed—we could beribbon all our main roads with flowering cherries; we could level thousands of acres of slag-heaps and turn them into vistas of delight; we could fill the land with the music of waterfalls. If I were dictator of this country the only permissible explosives would be reserved for the elimination—with a very few exceptions— of our public parks. These explosives would be so powerful that they would destroy every trace of the hundreds of thousands of triangular beds of blue lobelias by which we are at present assaulted, bring instant death to a million shocking-pink begonias, and send into a merciful coma, for an indefinite period, the armies of municipal officials who are entrusted by the State with the creation of these monstrosities. Then we could start again, from scratch, and there would be silence in the land. And the voice of Nichols would be heard, saying . . .

But we have strayed too far into the realm of fantasy. Let us get back to earth, meaning by 'earth' our own particular acre, or fraction of an acre, or whatever area we have managed to acquire.

There are only three ways in which a beautiful garden can be brought into being.

The first is through the eye of the gardener himself. If he has the eye, something of beauty may emerge. This is merely to say that in creating a garden we are creating—or endeavouring to create—a work of art. We are not merely filling in a blank space around the house, nor contriving a playground for tiny tots, nor providing ourselves with enough spinach for our old age.

(The word 'spinach' beckons me, for a moment, down yet another by-path. I see no reason why a vegetable garden should not be a thing of beauty in its own right; indeed, many a French *jardin potager* has great charm, melting into the garden proper, with the feathery plumes of the asparagus forming an airy background to the herbaceous border. If I ever created a vegetable garden I should begin by making an exhaustive study of the works of Cézanne, particularly the masterpieces of his middle period when he created such magical effects with cubes and triangles in various shades of green. One might produce designs of great excitement with stark oblongs of spinach and sharp triangles of lettuces, offset by bold splashes of purple beet, and dotted, here and there, with pink and magenta circles of ornamental cabbages. However, the Mrs Lewises of this world would probably regard such a scheme as impractical. Even if they were to adopt it they would almost certainly ruin the whole effect by going out and cutting a cabbage behind one's back.)

As we were saying, the first way in which a beautiful garden can be created is through the eye of the gardener himself. The second is through his feet.

The feet of the gardener are of first importance in garden design; indeed, without proper feet, attached to a pair of agile legs, it is difficult to see how a garden can be designed at all. In the past ten years, while my present garden has been coming into being, I reckon that I have walked at least 5000 miles. There are 3650 days in ten years. On most of these days I have wandered up and down, in and out, north, south, east and west, for at least an hour, and during the course of that hour I must have walked at least a mile and a half. One *has* to do this. How is it possible to assess the value —in shape, and colour, and general aesthetic significance— of a single branch of a single tree unless one has viewed it from every conceivable angle, in every condition of light and shade, at every time of the year? How can one plot the curve of a single bed unless one has pondered it, and continued to ponder it, time and again—gone to bed with it, dreamt about it? My friend and collaborator Mr Page is not exactly a willowy aesthete but when we are working together on—let us say—even a single branch of our trio of liquidambers he uses his secateurs with the delicacy of a master coiffeur adjusting the head-dress of a great lady.

But when all is said and done the greatest designer of any garden, once the main outline has been established, is Nature herself. That is the heaven of it and sometimes, I think, the hell. The gardener can provide the frame, set up his easel, and sketch the pattern, but as time marches on he must constantly step aside and hand over his brush to Nature. This can be agony, to see all his cherished concepts being so drastically modified by Nature's ruthless fingers, but it can also be ecstasy. As he looks over Nature's shoulder, watching the canvas change, wonderful things are happening. An apparently insignificant curve in a far corner suddenly assumes a dramatic importance, because Nature has decided to make a golden acacia grow at unprecedented speed, stretching out its glittering arms in a gesture that demands an audience. So the gardener rushes out to provide the audience, buying golden heathers to plant at the acacia's feet. Even as he is doing so, a couple of clematis are climbing into the pear tree, creating a carnival of colour which is so sensational that it must be cooled off by a glimmer of silver, so he rushes out again to buy a silver poplar. All over the garden, all through the year, Nature is slashing her brush all over the canvas, striking out new lines, hurrying and thrusting and pushing aside, dancing out of the frame, mocking, deriding, but always inspiring. Sometimes, when I look out of my bedroom window on a morning in May, and see that the *Clematis montana* is already sending a foam of pink blossom through the gutters, I wish that Nature would be still, just for a day or two, and let things stay as they are. Surely the picture is pleasing enough already? Surely we can take a rest? But no, says Nature. As if to prove her point she draws our attention to the fact that the wisteria has climbed up among the clematis, and that she has provided an exquisite tangle of rose and mauve, which demands immediate attention. 'Look what I have done!' says Nature, and having said it, drifts away on a sigh of the wind, leaving us to get on with the job of pruning, and wiring, and propping up ladders. It is as though a jeweller, bent over his bench, trying to make a necklace from a modest pile of diamonds and amethysts, were constantly being interrupted by a beautiful but boisterous female who unloaded sacks of rubies and emeralds all over the carpet. 'You *must* do something with these!' proclaims this mythical creature. And Nature says the same thing, in leaves and flowers. 'You *must* do something with these!' With the wild red poppies that she has scattered against the dark bronze background of the copper-beech. With the pale, ghostly ballets of wild white violets that she has evoked in the shadow of the silver pear. With a thousand twists and turns of leaf and petal, a thousand careless gestures of branch and blossom.

Making a garden, in short, is like a love affair. From which it follows that the only course for the really honest landscape gardener is to marry the owner, before he even begins to think of his design. And then, having married her, to tell her—politely but firmly— to *go away*.

CHAPTER THIRTEEN

GARDENING FOR THE ELDERLY

ALTHOUGH I am not yet of a pensionable age, time
marches on, and the day is not too distant when I
shall walk across the Common, cross the road, enter
the post office, and push a form across the counter in the
hopeful anticipation of receiving whatever may be due to me.

I have often thought about this day, as indeed one thinks
about death if one is sensible, and always with some embar-
rassment. When one goes along for the first time is it customary to indulge in polite conversation? Does one remark,
with feigned jocularity, that this is the first step to the grave?
But that might be tactless; there might be a very old gentleman just behind one, in a condition of even more advanced

senility, and he might regard such levity as ill-timed. Does the Postmistress lighten the occasion with a few facile compliments? Does she feign astonishment, and suggest that one cannot possibly be as old as all that, with all those teeth, and is there not, perhaps, some mistake in the date? This might happen, if she were of a friendly disposition, but if she were not, she might say something very different, like 'About time too'.

But what really worries me is the problem of facial expression, gesture, the movement of the hands, etc. It would be tempting to assume a lordly diffidence, to smile in a superior manner, and to stuff the notes in one's pocket, as though such a pittance were scarcely worth calling for. But it would also be unkind, for there might be old persons in the queue whose pensions were their sole means of support. So one must be seen to *want* the money, but how eagerly? To gaze at it hungrily, and to claw at it with trembling fingers, as though one were just about to rush across to the baker's for a packet of stale bread—this would be to overplay the part. It is all very difficult. When the time comes I think that I shall wait till it is dark and then slink in, modestly attired, and hope for the best.

But it will probably not be as bad as one thinks.

'Not as bad as one thinks.' This also applies to the problems of age in the garden. There must be thousands of gardeners, getting on in life, who are haunted by the fear of wha will happen when the shadows are lengthening on the lawn, when they can no longer stoop to weed, and when even the thought of climbing a ladder induces a feeling of vertigo. If they are rich the fears need not be quite so acute, for even in these days there is a small residue of persons masquerading as 'gardeners' who, if sufficiently bribed and cajoled, can be persuaded to do some of the heavy work, though they will almost certainly do it slowly and inefficiently, and only under the stimulus of phenomenal quantities of strong black tea. Still, they are better than nothing.

But what of the great majority, who can afford only a minimum of help? Although it may be 'not as bad as one thinks' it will be bad enough, and for those with large elaborate gardens that have been loved and tended over the years, the outlook is pretty grim. The greenhouses are falling to pieces, the ground-elder has got into the lily beds, the gutters round the out-houses are choked, and it is too cold to go out on the winter evenings armed with bracken to protect the tender buds of the camellias. For those in such a melancholy condition there is little to offer but the consolations of religion, which are considerable, but not sufficiently powerful to remove the plantains from the lawn.

Let us, therefore, in our survey of this problem, assume a married couple in their late fifties who have just bought their dream cottage in the country, to which they propose to retire in a few years' time, when their pensions mature. We will call them Mr and Mrs Langton-Jones, and I trust that there are no such persons in the flesh, armed with writs and waiting to pounce. They are filled with delight at the prospect awaiting them and being, as they fondly imagine, sensible persons, they have few apprehension of disaster. Everything will be so carefully planned that life will run like clockwork. There will be, of course, oil-fired central-heating. Such a comfort, and no trouble whatsoever. There will be a minimum of things to be dusted. There will be a dream kitchen, a washing-up machine, and every possible electrical apparatus. And by the time that the hall has been paved in tiles of plastic terra-cotta, the whole place will compare favourably with the more esteemed horrors of the Ideal Home Exhibition.

Then they start on the garden, motoring down at weekends, spending enchanted Saturdays and Sundays chopping down brambles—thereby ensuring that they will flourish with extra ferocity in the years to come—and digging up large clumps of rare montbretias under the mistaken impression that they are a form of grass. Mrs Langton-Jones hovers about in the background taking snapshots, eagerly looking forward to the day when she can show them to her friends with the phrase—which one seems to have heard before— 'It was a positive *wilderness* when we came!' When they return to London the boot of the car is filled with roses, cut with the new pair of secateurs, slashed in such a manner that they will almost certainly produce no more blossoms for at least three years.

This is the invariable procedure, followed by tens of thousands of charming, amiable people all over the world. In the faint hope that a few of them may be dissuaded from making some of the more elementary mistakes, let us imagine that we are accompanying Mr and Mrs Langton-Jones to their rural retreat on a summer week-end, let us watch what they are doing, and tell them, as precisely as possible, why they should not be doing it.

The cottage stands on rising ground in about half an acre of the aforesaid wilderness, and we do not need to make any very exhaustive survey of the garden to learn the first and most important thing about it; the soil is reasonably acid. There is a healthy rhododendron—a Pink Pearl by the look of it—growing in a corner near the ruined fowl-house, and a patch of bracken in a nearby field. Such things would not flourish if there were lime in the neighbourhood. Needless to say, the thought of examining the soil has never even occurred to the Langton-Joneses; they are the sort of inno-cents who would plant blue poppies on the white cliffs of Dover in a howling gale, and feel greatly pained when they withered away. However, they seem to have no lime troubles. If they should have, the best thing for them to do is to read Chapter Seven of this book, when they will find that these troubles, though they cannot be completely sur-mounted, can be greatly alleviated.

Now let us hover in the background and see what the Langton-Joneses are up to.

Says Mrs L.-J.: 'We *must* have a wisteria! Do you remem-ber that wisteria at Roquebrune?'

Mr L.-J. does indeed remember it. For it was at Roque-brune that they spent their honeymoon, and the scent of its blossom still drifts through the windows of his mind, on a breeze from the far-off South.

'It grows like mad,' urges Mrs L.-J. 'In a year or two it will be up to the roof.' She presses his hand: he smiles at her: there is a mellow glow of autumnal affection. It will be very pleasant to lie in bed on a May morning, watching the wisteria.

At this moment, Fate, from the distance, gives a hollow chuckle. For several reasons, which must now be explained.

Firstly, because in all probability the wisteria will *not* be 'up to the roof'. Paradoxically, the reason for this lies in the very speed of its growth; the young shoots sprout so swiftly that the wood has no time to harden. These shoots are of incredible delicacy; they can be fatally bruised if the wind knocks them against the wall, and mortally injured by clumsy fingers thrusting them under wall-nails. The fingers of the Langton-Joneses are almost certainly clumsy, and unless these dear people can be brought to realize that when they are training their wisteria they are dealing with material so sensitive that it would like to be wrapped in cotton-wool, they will watch the years go by with scarcely any progress at all.

My own way with wisteria is to allow the young shoots to advance for at least three feet from the last nail, or wire, or whatever may be supporting them, and then, scarcely touching them, holding my breath, and addressing a brief but earnest admonition to the Almighty, coax them into position with a finger-nail.

If the Langton-Joneses will follow these instructions— including the admonition to the Almighty, which is of first importance—they may get their wisteria up to the roof.

At which point, Fate will give another hollow chuckle.

For, having got up to the roof, the wisteria will proceed to get into the gutters, at even greater speed than before. Once it has got into the gutters it has a habit of taking hold, and if it is not checked, it will have the gutters down. You may suggest that I am assuming very little intelligence on the part of the L.-J.s, and that people who cannot be bothered to control a single creeper do not deserve to have any creepers at all. Which is quite true, but somewhat unkind. This, remember, is their first wisteria; they rejoice in its growth, and when they see it climbing high they let it enjoy itself. Besides, Mr L.-J. is no longer very good at climbing ladders.

This ladder business is really the heart of the matter. Elderly people should not be allowed to climb ladders, and if their friends see them attempting to do so they should give them a sharp tug so that they fall off before their feet touch thè second rung. Again, you may suggest that I am crediting the L.-J.s with very little self-control. This is quite true, but quite irrelevant. A ladder is a lure, a standing temptation, whatever one's age, as I know to my cost. In the course of every year there are storms and tempests and freak commotions in which things are blown away from walls, and if there is nobody else at hand there is nothing to be done but swallow a swift dry martini, hurry to the tool-shed, drag out the ladder, prop it up on the wall, climb up it, and fall off. In my own case this has happened time and again, sometimes with very painful results, and it has nothing whatever to do with the dry martini.

At inordinate length we seem to have established one fundamental principle for elderly gardeners; they must eliminate ladders from their lives, once and for all, and confine their climbing activities to a pair of steps. Does this mean that they can never rejoice in a wisteria? No. For with a pair of steps they can reach up to the lower sill of the first floor windows. Under these they can trail horizontal wires for the wisteria to climb along, and if it shows any signs of wanting to go any higher—as it will—they must simply chop off the growths, preferably in the very early spring before the flower-buds begin to form, for these are almost as easily damaged as the young shoots of the branches. Very long shoots can also be cut back at the end of August to encourage flowering in the following year.

Before saying good-bye to this most exquisite and exotic of all creepers, I should like to recommend two varieties of especial beauty which are all too seldom grown. The first is *Wisteria floribunda macrobotrys*, which has tassels more than twice as long as the common *Wisteria sinensis*, of an even more delicate shade of mauve and equally floriferous. The second is the white *Wisteria venusta*. This is not quite as hardy as the others and does best against a south wall. Nor does it grow quite so quickly. But its white is so immaculate, and it is so sweetly scented, that it is worth waiting for, even if the years in which it will delight you are all too few.

Finally, although the wisterias riot all over the Mediterranean, where they often have to go for weeks without rain, in this country you cannot overdo the watering.

We left the L.-J.s wandering round their wilderness, taking snapshots and dreaming dreams, and we set ourselves the unkind task of suggesting that one of those dreams, at least, might not be so easy to realize as they imagine.

Let us try to make amends by suggesting some of the varieties of wall-covering that may be specially recommended for the elderly—using the world 'elderly' to indicate all those who have been sensible enough to chop up their ladders and use them for firewood to warm their stiffening limbs.

High up on the list I would put the large family of the japonicas (the genus of ornamental quinces which are related to the pears, the crabs and the medlars). The charming name 'japonica', which has blossomed on the pages of Victorian novels and fallen gently from the lips of generations of nice old ladies wandering through the shrubberies of their stately homes, has been discarded by the botanists. We are now instructed to call them chaenomeles, which sounds like something to do with the gnomes of Zurich. I shall continue to call them japonicas, except when I order them from the nurseries. This is not only a matter of euphony but of common courtesy. When I am showing some nice but not very knowledgeable woman round my garden, when she sees a sheet of coral flaming on the wall (repeat 'sheet'), and when she exclaims that she has never seen such a beautiful 'japonica' before, in which assertion she will probably be correct, it would be churlish to correct her and mutter 'chaenomeles' even if one could remember it and, having remembered it, pronounce it.

There are at least a hundred things to be said in favour of the japonicas. I will say only a few of them, keeping an eye on the L.-J.s.

Firstly, they can be planted in almost any sort of soil, including lime. The 'experts' would qualify this statement and even so delightful and knowledgeable a writer as Edward Hyams states that they 'do best in well-drained but moisture-retaining loam'. To which I can only retort that my own japonicas, which are spectacular, are planted against an east wall with their roots under a concrete pavement, in a bed nine inches wide, which gets so dry in the summer that the soil resembles brick-dust.

Secondly, although they grow at a reasonable speed—about eighteen inches a year—they have a convenient habit of stopping when they reach about eight feet, so that Mr L.-J. will not have to venture further than the second rung of his pair of steps.

Thirdly, they are very easy to prune. I have never been a good pruner and invariably leave the roses to the unerring fingers of Mr Page. But with the japonicas it is merely a question of snipping off the bits that stick out too far, and allowing oneself the occasional indulgence of cutting a small spray for indoors.

Fourthly, they have a long flowering period. In this year of writing (1967) they were spangled with blossom in mid-

February, were still blooming in April, and even staged occasional return visits in May, like *prima donnas* who, having already made a large number of 'Farewell Tours', announce their 'Positively Last Appearance'.

Fifthly, their foliage remains green and perky through the summer months, and some of them—such as *Chaenomeles japonica* Boule de Feu—have attractive yellow fruits, like their nearest relatives, the quinces. These are highly recommended by nurserymen and gardening writers for making jelly. I cannot share their enthusiasm. The only time I ever tasted japonica jelly I felt that its proper place was in the medicine cupboard, to be used as an emergency emetic.

Here are five of the loveliest and easiest japonicas, at about 12s. 6d. each:

Chaenomeles speciosa Moerloesii. Commonly known as 'Apple-Blossom', a title which explains itself. Pink-cheeked fruit.

Chaenomeles speciosa Crimson and Gold. Another self-explanatory title. Very large flowers, very rich crimson petals, bright gold anthers.

Chaenomeles speciosa Cameo. A new variety, which might well have been called 'Peach Blossom'.

Chaenomeles japonica alpina. Perhaps the most freely flowering of the lot, with brick-red blossom that clashes superbly against an old brick wall.

Chaenomeles speciosa Snow. The best of the pure whites.

It is to be hoped that the L.-J.s, by now, will have got the message, will have burned their ladders, and even in the matter of their pair of steps, made quite sure that none of the rungs are rickety. It is also to be assumed that the walls of their cottage are still mostly bare, in spite of all these raptures about the japonicas. How shall they clothe these walls? An answer to that question would stretch to many volumes. I will merely make a few 'ladder-proof' suggestions, which are not likely to occur to the average beginner.

One of the great problems is the north wall. This is the side of the house which is usually most neglected, and yet it is also the side which most needs covering, for the simple reason that here, as often as not, are situated the least attractive outbuildings. Why do so few people bother about this section of their domain? Presumably because they imagine that it does not get enough sun. But this is a mistaken impression. The number of creepers that flourish in the shade may not be as large as the number that rejoice in the sunshine, but it is still impressive.

Consider the roses. Here is a list of roses which have grown in my own gardens on walls which received no sunshine whatsoever, and for this very reason lasted longer in full flower than if they had been scorched in a southern aspect: Allan Chandler. This is a sensational single rose for the dark places, of a rich crimson, with petals three to four inches across, and a central boss of brilliant yellow stamens.

Gloire de Dijon. The rose of one's grandparents, whose ivory and apricot beauty seems to be untarnished by the years, holding its own against all newcomers.

Paul's Lemon Pillar and Madame Albert Carrière. These are both white roses, though the former, as its name suggests, is very faintly tinged with green.

A moment ago we mentioned unattractive outbuildings. Here I must put in a word for that greatly neglected genus of creepers—the ivies. The ivy seems to have been born to be misunderstood. There are still thousands of people who harbour the strange illusion that if it climbs up the bark of

H

a tree it acts as a parasite, sucking away the vital sap and eventually destroying the tree. The ivy has no such unpleasant characteristics; its tendrils are quite harmless, and it obtains its nourishment, like any other creeper, from the earth in which it is planted. True, if it is neglected for several decades it will do considerable damage to a wall, but as our friends the Langton-Joneses will be centenarians before this happens, they can perhaps view the prospect with equanimity. However, if they have tender feelings about posterity, they can plant it on a trellis. Again, there are all too many people whose knowledge of the ivies is confined to the common *Hedera Helix*, which creates a somewhat melancholy mood. They should learn, and learn quickly, that there are ivies which hold the sunshine in their leaves, ivies that reflect the moonlight, and ivies that suggest the dappled half-lights of a forest glade. Here are three for their attention:

Hedera Helix Jubilee. This has a very warm place in my heart for my own specimen was given to me by one of the grand old ladies of British gardening, Mrs Gwendolyn Anley, on her eightieth birthday. It is a dark ivy whose leaves have a golden centre, and it has flourished as though it were eager to be worthy of her.

Hedera Helix Glacier. A delicate small-leaved variety, of an almost iridescent silver, particularly effective against a white wall.

Hedera colchica dentata variegata. Bold leaves with splashes of yellow as bright as primroses.

Still lingering in the shadows of our northern walls let us make a brief list of a few more 'ladderless' climbers for this part of the house. (The more favoured aspects we will leave to the tender mercies of Mr and Mrs Langton-Jones. They will almost certainly do everything wrong, with the utmost enthusiasm, but one of the greatest rewards of gardening is to be found in profiting from one's own mistakes.)

Garrya elliptica. This Californian evergreen is not, strictly speaking, a climber, but it can be persuaded to act as such with a minimum of wall-nails. I mention it because it not only tolerates deep shade but actually prefers it, and also because its crowning hour is in the depth of winter. It begins to flower in mid-January, covering itself with pale greeny-yellow catkins, twice as long as the common 'lambs' tails' which hang in the hedgerows. Of all the winter-flowering shrubs this is the one which, to me, gives the most welcome foretaste of the coming of spring.

Hydrangea petiolaris. The finest specimen of this climber in Britain is to be seen in the Savill Gardens near Windsor, climbing up a stately oak to a height of over fifty feet. This might suggest that it can scarcely be included in the 'ladder-less' class, but it can easily be trained horizontally as soon as it shows signs of getting beyond the reach of the steps. For those who love hydrangeas—there are some people who have a strange aversion to them—this climbing variety should have great charm. The flowers are pure white, with an irregular margin of large sterile flowers round a packed centre of fertile ones. They begin to star the walls in June and last well into September.

Clematis macropetala. Here I resume my battle with the 'experts' who, when discussing the clematis, have a habit of talking a great deal of nonsense. For years they have been telling us to plant the *macropetala* in full sunshine and since I am of humble and compliant disposition I followed their advice, with the most depressing results. The lovely bell-shaped flowers faded almost before they had time to open and the colour, which should have been a rich shade of plum,

came out as a sickly slate. One day, surveying this sad prospect, something told me that it was, of its very nature, a
flower of the shadows, and that it wanted, as it were, to lead
a secret and secluded life, far from the light of day. So when
the autumn came we transplanted it to a dark corner where
no gleam of sunshine ever penetrated, and the winter had
scarcely passed before it was burgeoning into leaf, and
climbing the wall with its delicate fingers. And in April its
bells were ringing out their dark music. This is a clematis
for all the seasons of life but especially, I think, for the elderly.
The young might pass it by, but the elderly can stand in
front of it, or sit, if they are so inclined, and gaze and—if it
does not sound too fanciful—listen.

There are so many other varieties of clematis which will
flourish in the shade, including the popular *montana rubens*,
that I will not attempt to list them. As for suggesting 'hints
about cultivation', the best tip I can give is to make an
earnest study of the advice of all the 'experts', and then do
precisely the opposite.

We have faced the problem of climbing; let us now face
the problem of stooping.

When I was a very young man, in the *Down the Garden Path*
days, one of the greatest joys of my first garden lay in the fact
that I could share it with my mother. She was a country
woman through and through, who had been condemned to
end her days in London; when she spoke wistfully of the
country—against a background of grimy plane trees in
Cambridge Square—she meant what she called 'real
country'. Real country, to her, meant a garden that merged
into fields, which were bounded by deep, mysterious woods

and distant hills. Real country meant that the nearest contact with the world was a little railway station at least five
miles from the house, with only one train a day. Real country
meant water from the well, and eggs from the farm, and
muddy lanes decked with wild roses. It bore not the faintest
resemblance to the stockbroker-belt, its roads had never seen
a bus or a charabanc and it was quite innocent of anything
remotely resembling a golf-course.

But most of all, 'real country' meant getting out to the
garden in a very old skirt, with a mat in one hand and a fork
in the other, bending down and weeding. And this was precisely what my mother had been forbidden to do. She had
very high blood pressure, and the family doctor had told her
that, with her heart condition, she was 'walking around with
a bomb in her pocket'—a remark which she used to quote
with a curious unconcern, as though it were faintly amusing.
But how was she to be prevented from stooping? It was as
difficult for her to ignore a weed in a flower-bed as to pass a
baby in its pram, particularly if the baby was crying and if
its nanny was not giving it proper attention. A walk through
the Park with my mother ended, only too often, in baby
trouble. And a walk through the garden ended, almost invariably, in her bending down or stooping, before there
was time to stop her.

It was with this problem in mind that I contrived the
little rock-garden by the pond, though 'rock-garden' is not
quite the right expression for so singular an experiment. For
it was really nothing more than a large mound of earth that
had been chucked into the field while the pond was being
dug. Even if it had not been for her, the pond would have
been made (the reader is by now acquainted with my views
on water in the garden). But the design of the pond, or rather

of the mound which came out of it, was created for her special benefit. It was very steep, surrounded by a cinder path which prevented her shoes from getting wet. It had a minimum of rocks, partly because I could not afford them, and partly because they would have looked ridiculous in a cottage garden. And it had, I am thankful to say, a great many weeds, all of which could be easily pulled up by hand with no stooping whatsoever. I should be the last to claim that it was a masterpiece of landscaping, but I loved it. For it became my mother's particular province in which she spent many happy hours, feeling that she was doing something really useful, breathing in the sweet country air, and when she was tired, sitting down on a little camp-stool, and watching the antics of the tadpoles, the newts, the beetles and all the other mysterious denizens of the water. Like myself she often wondered 'where they came from'. I have yet to learn the answer to that question.

This strange eminence, obviously, could not be reproduced in many gardens; it arose from special circumstances and, although it was somewhat bizarre, it seemed to fit into the lie of the land. But there are other anti-stooping devices which the elderly might consider, such as the creation of long walls, about three feet high, hollowed at the top, and filled with soil to a depth of a foot, in which many charming plants will flourish. Unfortunately, unless the elderly are also rather rich, they may be inclined to build their walls of breeze blocks, which are of singular repulsion. They would be far better advised to make enquiries from the local authorities and lay in a store of broken paving stones, which are cheap and easy to come by in most parts of the country. However, please do not ask me what I mean by 'local authorities'. They vary according to one's temperament and way of life.

On the various occasions when I have needed them I have been deluged with paving stones a few days after dropping a hint at the village pub. But the postman can also be helpful, and also the dustbin men, and in the last resort one can go to the Town Hall, provided that one is prepared to spend a great deal of time explaining, to begin with, that one is neither an expectant mother nor in immediate need of national assistance.

Here is a brief list of things for planting at the base of a wall. None of them will grow too high.

Hedera Helix Cavendishii. This is a very tightly-growing, closely-packed ivy, flecked with silver, which in time will conceal the bricks completely. For my own part, I would be quite content to cover the entire wall in this manner; I have seen it done in a Jersey garden, with the happiest results. But if the Langton-Joneses want more variety, they must certainly invest in . . .

Cotoneaster adpressa and *C. Dammeri.* These are as nearly ever-green as makes no matter, and adapt themselves to walls so tidily that they look as though they had been carefully nailed and trained, whereas in fact they need no attention whatsoever. They have several other endearing qualities; in the summer they are great favourites with the bees, whose peregrinations can be observed by the elderly, with suitably poignant thoughts, and in the autumn they are covered with brilliant scarlet berries. These, in their turn, attract the birds, thereby suggesting yet another diversion for the elderly, who can sit on the wall and shoo them away. Finally, they seldom grow more than three feet tall; if they grow any taller they can easily be snipped off without being made to look untidy.

The Langton-Joneses might also feel inclined to invest in a Virginia creeper, which they can train horizontally. Not with the aid of wires, for it is self-clinging, but simply by coaxing it with their fingers. Although it is not evergreen its luxurious stem patterns will soften the harshness of the breeze blocks even in the depths of winter. For a low wall such as this I would suggest a small-leaved form which is not too rampant, in particular the ponderously named *Parthenocissus tricuspidata* (syn. *Vitis inconstans*).

That will be enough for our friends to be getting on with. If they demand more, as I hope they will, they must study the nurserymen's catalogues, which will give them plenty of ideas, or—better still—go for walks and look over the hedges into the gardens of their neighbours.

We have dealt with the problem of climbing; we have dealt with the problem of stooping; let us now, calling a spade a spade, deal with the problem of sweating.

Elderly people really should not sweat. They should stop it. I know that there are a great many health magazines which extol the benefits of this natural function in almost lyrical terms, and that there are a great many city gentlemen who swear by Sauna baths, where they congregate after luncheon in order to sit on marble slabs, like obscene balloons, glaring at each other through a veil of hideous dew. But oddly enough the readers of health magazines seldom look very healthy, and the city gentlemen always seem to reach the obituary columns while they are still in the sixties. The healthiest human being I ever knew was a lady of the old school who would have swooned at the very mention of the word 'sweat'—the word 'perspiration' would probably have killed her outright—and she died with great cheerfulness at the age of ninety-eight, encased in whalebone and smothered in deodorants.

The greatest sweat-inducer in the garden is the lawn, and the Langton-Joneses—if I know them at all, and I seem to be getting to know them pretty well—will certainly make the lawn the centre of their design. 'Everybody' has a lawn and 'everybody', of course, must be right.

But . . . the elderly?

Here I would like to take you to the window and show you a picture which, I hope, will point a moral. It is a morning in early spring, and in the centre of the lawn stands Mr Page, the gardener. He is surrounded by an assortment of turves, in various geometrical patterns, which he is about to insert, with mathematical precision, into patches of bare earth. These patches mark the places where, yesterday, he removed slabs of that rampant grass which is popularly known as 'Yorkshire Fog'. It seeds itself on the winds that blow over the wall from the Common, and unless we kept our eyes open it would eventually smother the whole domain.

If we walked downstairs and out into the garden—continuing to watch Mr Page—we should note that the grass on which we are treading is powdered with peat, which he applied last week, lugging it across from the tool-shed in bags weighing half a hundredweight, and spreading it with considerable delicacy. Lawns are not just patches of mown grass; they hunger and they thirst; sometimes my own lawn hungers and thirsts to such an extent that I wonder how long I shall be able to go on satisfying its demands. Moreover, every lawn has its own personality. My lawn demands peat because it grows on a light sandy soil; if we were on heavy clay we should have been treating it with sharp sand, to help the drainage; if we had been on lime . . . but that is too long a story.

Approaching nearer to Mr Page, we observe that by his

side is a sack of Velvetone—the spring formula—which like the peat comes in half-hundredweight sacks, is applied dry, and watered in.

But this is only the beginning of the story, only one of a whole album of pictures that I might reveal to you concerning the dealings of the remarkable Mr Page with his perfect lawn. For though I have to pay for the darned thing it is through his intelligence and—elderly, please note—his sweat, that it has come into being. Of all these pictures perhaps the most intimidating is the one which shows him raking the lawn in the autumn, bending over it grimly and dragging the sharp prongs over the surface to remove the dead matter that accumulates during the year. The amount of stuff he manages to get away is remarkable, forming a pile several feet deep, which has to be wheeled away and dumped in the annexe. Of all the manifold duties connected with the lawn this is one of the most important and also one of the most fatiguing. After twenty minutes of grass-raking most elderly persons, if they went about it with the same energy as Mr Page, would certainly be totally exhausted and quite possibly dead.

And we are *still* only at the beginning of it all, for we have not even mentioned the mowing, on hot summer afternoons, nor the piling of the grass into the barrow and the shovelling of it on to the compost heap, nor the inordinate amount of weeding—demanding very sharp eyes as well as a very supple back—which must be done by hand. Nor any of the subtler and more delicate activities which demand not only brawn but brain, particularly as the lawn advances towards perfection. A lawn, we must always remember, is not a natural creation; it is a luxurious artifice, which must be expensively fed and elaborately cosseted. A perfect lawn is a pampered lawn; and pampered lawns, like pampered people, are apt to develop a number of tiresome diseases. They might almost be called 'digestive' diseases. To give only one example out of many, there is the fungus called *Fusarium nivale*, which comes as patches of white mould towards the end of the summer. Most people who saw this on their lawns for the first time would have no idea what it was, nor how they ought to deal with it. For their information, they should treat it with Merfusan, a mercury compound which is applied dry around the edges to prevent it from spreading. But they might read a great many articles on lawns before discovering that such a disease even existed.

So what are the elderly to do, failing the services of Mr Page, which—as long as I have anything to say in the matter —will be rigorously denied them?

The quick and easy answer to this question is that they should not have a lawn at all. If the time ever comes when I have to leave my present garden, for reasons of health, for reasons of money, for any of the many reasons which Fate may have up her sleeve, I shall retreat deeper into the country, and retire to the shelter of some small dwelling surrounded by fields with an acre or so of wild garden which will remain, ostensibly, wild, though in fact it will of course be nothing of the sort. In the apparently rustic hedgerows I shall plant the exquisite *Rubus* Tridel, which looks like the sort of blackberry one might encounter in the Elysian fields, and by its side there will be *Rosa spinosissima*, which might be described as a common dog-rose after a trip to the beauty specialist. In the orchard there will be drifts of February Gold, which to me is the most rewarding of all the smaller daffodils, earlier, of a purer, paler colour, and astonishingly prolific, increasing annually in the toughest, coarsest grass.

It is a daffodil that Wordsworth might have encountered in his wanderings, and immortalized in an extra couplet. That is the kind of garden that I should try to create, with a country pond gleaming through the apple trees, a pond in which I should plant no lilies, but only the wild water-hawthorne, a pond whose banks would rustle with the *Iris foetidissima*, which would also, perhaps, shelter a friendly family of moorhens. You may think it all sounds rather a mess. So do I. You may also think that it might prove, in the end, to be rather expensive. So do I. Everything always is, particularly everything informal. To achieve an elegant informality in the garden always costs the earth. But it would be worth it, even if the moorhens had to be imported from Outer Mongolia, as is all too probable. It would be worth it for the simple reason that one would never quite know what was going to happen next. And for the old in years, not to know what is going to happen next is one of the surest ways of keeping young in heart.

The only certain thing about this dream garden is that there would be no lawn. When one has known perfection it is wiser to have nothing at all than to try to accept the second-best.

But I am not the Langton-Joneses, and it is fairly certain that if they were told that they could have no lawn at all they would feel cheated, and lose heart, and begin to sulk. Besides, what would the neighbours say? Everybody has a lawn and people would think it very odd if they did not have one. They would think that there must be something nasty in the wood-shed if they did not have a lawn.

Very well, the Langton-Joneses shall have their lawn, but it will not be a grass lawn. It will be a lawn of *Chamaemelum nobile*—the fragrant low-growing carpeting plant which

needs scarcely any mowing, and can be kept in order, particularly on sandy soils, merely by walking on it. As this is a
somewhat revolutionary idea, I would suggest that before
they put it into practice they should pay a visit to the glorious
gardens of Sissinghurst Castle, in Kent, where they will find
a chamomile lawn in perfect condition, flanked by paving
stones and bounded by yew hedges, a green and growing
memorial to its creator, the late Victoria Sackville-West.
They can also study chamomile in its wild condition around
the cliffs of Cornwall and on many downlands of the British
Isles. When their eyes first light on such a lawn they may
experience a faint feeling of disappointment, for admittedly
it has not the smooth, velvety beauty of the perfect grass lawn.
But how many grass lawns actually *have* this 'smooth,
velvety beauty'? How many are free from plantains, from
couch grass, from daisies, from clover, from moss, and from
all the diseases to which the lawn is heir? When did they last
see one? Have they ever seen one at all? If they have visited
my own garden, and seen Mr Page's lawn, they will be able
to answer the last question with a cheerful affirmative. But
if they have read the foregoing pages, they will realize at
what a cost of time and money and effort it has been created.

A chamomile lawn does not demand all that time—within
a couple of years it will begin to come into its own. Nor does
it demand all that money. As for effort, it needs no weeding,
for it smothers all intruders—though after it has produced
its attractive little white daisy heads in the summer, the
flowers should be cut off by hand. But this is surely a task
that should not intimidate the elderly, who can sit themselves
down on it and pick gently away at it, with no greater effort
than if they were knitting. And of course it needs no mowing
—you 'mow' it, as it were, simply by walking on it. Obvi-

ously, you cannot treat it as a parade-ground, and it might look rather sorry for itself for a few days if you were to give a garden-party on it. Otherwise, it has no serious drawbacks that I know of.

And always, there is this exquisite asset of the scent, an aroma with a faint suggestion of lemon tea, so fragrant that if the Langton-Joneses' neighbours had cherished any thoughts about unpleasant objects in the tool-shed, they would be filled with sweetness and charity after a single stroll across it.

There are several other varieties of scented lawns which might interest our friends. Those who live on chalky soils might consider a lawn of thyme, in particular *Thymus Drucei* and *Thymus Herba-barona* (the caraway thyme). On damp soils they are more likely to succeed with the tiny *Mentha Requienii*, with minute flowers and leaves, barely half an inch tall, flavoured with a pungent aroma of peppermint. All have much to be said in their favour, though not perhaps as much as the chamomile, for—in my experience at least— they are apt to develop bare patches and to vary greatly in growth according to the degree of sunshine available. But if the elderly will only consider them, and make a little effort, and write to the nice people whom I have listed in the appendix, they will find that they may be able to walk across their own lawns, and to console themselves with the thought that —even at the end of the chapter—all the fragrance has not yet gone out of life.

Before we leave this section I would like to say a word about mechanical aids to labour-saving in the garden, with a special eye on the elderly. These devices are constantly getting into the news. Only recently I attended an exhibition which adjured us to 'Take the Back-ache out of Gardening'. The centre of attraction was a very expensive lawn-mower with a seat attached. It was an instrument of fiendish power and it was exercising a compulsive attraction upon an old lady, who had got as far as asking if she could buy it by instalments. Evidently, she saw herself reclining on it, gently drifting round her smooth-shaven lawns, warbling 'Greensleeves' and occasionally waving a dainty hand to her envious neighbours. This charming vision, I longed to warn her, was unlikely to materialize. If she got the thing to go at all it would immediately take command and propel her down the drive at forty miles an hour, and out into the High Street, leaving a trail of death and destruction in her wake.

There never has and never will be any way of 'taking the back-ache' out of gardening and unless we accept this fact we had better give up gardening altogether. This does not mean that science has had absolutely nothing to contribute. In the field of weed-killers and pesticides, for example, the scientists have done a great deal. If they do much more they will almost certainly wipe out not only the weeds and the pests but the entire human race. However, this is by the way, and I only mention it to remind you that these things should be handled with gloves on, in more senses than one. And even if your tool-shed contained enough lethal mixtures to poison the entire state of New York, your garden would still present you with a large number of weeds that can only be eliminated by hand. My own garden is a case in point. Every spring it is assailed by winged battalions of sycamore seeds, blown by the wind from the trees on the Common, which were planted some fifty years ago by somebody who must have had a standing grudge against all gardeners. These

invaders intrude into every nook and cranny, seeding themselves between the cracks in the paving stones, taking up
their positions in the centre of closely packed clumps of
thyme, and even blocking up the gutters under the roof.
Except in open places where they can be hoed, every one
of them must be removed by hand.

The main contribution of the gadget-makers, in my own
opinion, has been in the redesigning of a few essential tools
and in the elimination of a certain amount of weight. These
tools are best chosen personally, for every elderly gardener
has his individual problems, whether they are arthritic or
horticultural. But no gardener of any age wants to burden
himself with unnecessary weight, which is why we should
be so grateful for the invention of plastic wheelbarrows and
plastic watering-cans.

Finally, we come to the greatest problem of all . . . Time.
Our friends Mr and Mrs Langton-Jones still have plenty of
this unpurchasable commodity, for they are only fifty-five,
with a reasonable expectation of being able to plant slow-
growing trees without expiring before they reach some sort
of maturity. But for those who are in their mid-sixties—and
this is an age when thousands of hard-working couples enter
into their first green inheritance—what about them? Is it
all too late? Is it worth trying at all?

The problem does not affect myself, because I have every
intention of continuing to plant things up to the very last
moment. Even when the hearse has drawn up to the door
and the horses are champing at the bit—it would be nice to
have horses—some part of me will be in the garden, planting
tulip-trees which will not produce many tulip-flowers until

A.D. 2000. This is, of course, a matter of temperament, and one's personal creed. I have an obstinate belief—illogical, sentimental but deeply held—that when I have planted a tree something of me goes into the roots and abides in the tree as the years pass on, rising with the sap and dwelling in the leaves and the branches. For a bachelor, it is a comforting creed.

But for those who do not cherish such illusions—if illusions they be?

Let us return to the practical. Let us assume that you are sixty-five, that you have just retired to your first house with a garden and—to make things really difficult—let us imagine that you are faced with one of the most intractable problems of all, for those who do not live in the heart of the country, the problem of screening, by which, of course, we mean shutting out the people next door. However charming our neighbours may be we don't want them on top of us. In America, of course, they feel differently about this. When an American suburban housewife is planning a garden her first concern is to ensure that the people next door have a clear and uninterrupted view into her bathroom; to attempt to screen it off, even by the most modest of deciduous shrubs, would be regarded, in some subtle way, as undemocratic. I do not wish to peer into other people's bathrooms; I should be greatly offended if they peered into mine; and I am assuming that our sixty-five-year-old couple—we will call them Mr and Mrs Peebles-Smith—share the same unneighbourly sentiments.

But what do they *do* about it? A great many things, and quickly. The first thing they do is of a negative nature. They banish from their minds all thought of poplars. When people begin to garden—this applies to the young as well as to the

223

old—and when they want a tree that grows quickly, as they always do, their minds fly like homing pigeons to poplars, usually to the ubiquitous Lombardy poplar (*Populus nigra italica*) which casts so welcome a shade on the long straight roads of France. A visit to the nurseryman informs them that they can buy excellent specimens of this tree, ten feet high, for 22s. 6d. Even at ten feet, a row of these trees cunningly planted along the bottom wall will blot out a large part of the neighbours' bathroom. (We will call the neighbours Mr and Mrs Fenwick-Robinson.) And even if the trees do not entirely obscure the bathroom, they will cast a merciful shadow over Mrs Fenwick-Robinson's bust, which, as far as Mrs Peebles-Smith is concerned, is the principal object in need of screening.

I have nothing against poplars in their proper place. A cluster of silver poplars in a coppice is a very lovely sight, evoking the ghost of Corot, and it is made even lovelier if it links branches with a group of golden poplars—*Populus serotina aurea*. As for the scented poplar *Populus trichocarpa*, this gives us one of the sweetest fragrances of spring, when the sun is shining on its sticky, aromatic leaves. But the proper place for poplars is not against a wall in a suburban garden. If Mrs Peebles-Smith will take the trouble to look in her nurseryman's catalogue she will find that the Lombardy poplar 'makes a striking avenue if planted 20 feet apart. Height 100 to 120 feet'. And if she will credit the nurseryman with knowing his own business she will realize that she will only be able to plant, at most, six poplars, unless she is going to crowd them to death, and that through the gaps in this so-called screen the bust of Mrs Fenwick-Robinson will still be clearly visible, for years to come.

Although I said that I had 'nothing against' poplars there

are, in fact, several things to be said against them. They have very aggressive roots, and because of their rapid growth they need exceptionally strong stakes, preferably of steel tubing driven three feet into the soil. This is not a job to be done by the elderly. Again, they are not too happy in the neighbourhood of cities, where they have a habit of developing mysterious diseases. Have you ever seen a really fine group of poplars in a city park? But their principal drawback is that they are deciduous, almost aggressively deciduous, shaking off the last hint of leafage in October and remaining gaunt and naked till the following May.

At this point we take out our pencils and write the word 'conifers'. If you think that I am going to ask you to plant a row of the common Lawson's cypress you would be greatly mistaken. For the next thing we write is *Cupressocyparis Leylandii*.

The Leyland cypress, as we will call it for the sake of simplicity, is God's gift to screeners, and only God knows why it is so seldom used. When people first meet it in my garden, soaring upwards in its dark feathery masses, they find it quite impossible to believe that it has been planted for so short a time. I try to explain to them that one of the reasons for its Jack-and-the-beanstalk quality lies in the fact it contains the 'blood', if we may so call it, of the equally fast-growing *Cupressus macrocarpa*, which, alas, is only hardy in sheltered places by the sea. I also explain that it has only gone ahead at this pace because it was properly planted, staked and watered. But people obviously do not believe me; they merely raise their eyebrows, and think that I am pulling the long bow. If they make any comment at all, it is to the effect that it must have been a gigantic size when I put it in.

In that last observation lies a very dangerous fallacy.

Mrs Peebles-Smith should *not* buy gigantic trees. She should buy small pot plants, for the simple reason that in a couple of years they will have caught up with the giants and, after that, will probably grow twice as fast and twice as strong. This is one of the elementary facts about gardening that people, especially elderly people, will not get into their heads. Transplanting a mature tree is a major surgical operation, a violent shock to the nervous and physical system. (Anybody who doubts that a tree has a nervous system should spend the rest of his life in a factory, making plastic acorns.) This shock can often be fatal, but even if the tree recovers, the period of convalescence will be protracted, and during this period the young, pot-grown tree will be forging briskly ahead, and before we know where we are it will have outstripped its elders.

Let us therefore assume that Mrs Peebles-Smith, for once in a way, listens to advice, and that she invests in a dozen *Cupressocyparis Leylandii*, which will be more than enough to screen a fifty-foot boundary. They will cost her seven guineas a dozen at the time of writing, and if she turns to the appendix she will find out where to get them. The fact that they are grown in pots means that she can get them at any time of the year—Midsummer's Eve, if she feels so inclined—and this is in itself a saving of time. When they arrive she should plant them in four groups of three, at a distance of not less than four feet from each other and three feet from the wall; the ground, of course, will have been previously prepared, there will be plenty of peat at hand to scatter round the roots, and the stakes will already have been driven in.

And the whole thing will look like hell. For what, in fact, do we see at the end of all this caper? We see a dozen spindly little objects stuck in the ground with a dozen stakes towering above them. We are rather tired, we are minus seven guineas—and a good deal more, when we add the peat and the stakes and the labour—and we are beginning to feel our age. Sixty-five. Why did we start on this ridiculous adventure? Why did we ever listen to Nichols? Above all, what do we do?

What we do is to continue to listen to Nichols. We prepare to spend still more money and we copy out the following list:

Chamaecyparis Lawsoniana. Next to the Leyland, the fastest-growing.

Cupressus arizonica conica. Silver-grey, slender and swift.

Chamaecyparis Lawsoniana lutea. The brightest of all the golden cypresses.

For still further colour variation, a group of . . .

Ilex Aquifolium. The variegated hollies, of which Silver Queen and Golden King are the outstanding examples.

We choose specimens of about two to three feet high, and when they arrive, preferably in October, the drill for planting will be the same as before. The important thing to remember is to plant them in irregular groups *in front* of the Leyland cypresses, because although they will be taller and more substantial when they arrive, in a couple of years the Leylands will have outstripped them.

And the end product of all this? The end product will be a tapestry of dark green, shot with gold and grey and silver, growing every year more beautiful, more rich in substance and—how shall I say?—more protective.

'By which time,' observes Mrs Peebles-Smith tersely, 'I shall almost certainly be dead.' Which, of course, is possible. For that matter, she may drop dead before she reaches the end of this chapter, and if it goes on much longer, so may I.

However, Mrs P.-S. is really being rather pessimistic. Her 'tapestry' will be well over the top of the wall before she says good-bye to her sixties. And it will not be just a commonplace 'screen'; it will be an object of beauty in its own right, glowing with colours as subtly exciting as any in the garden.

However, there is some justification for Mrs P.-S.'s objections and admittedly we seem to have provided her with a somewhat gloomy prospect for several years to come. So here is a suggestion by which her life may be considerably brightened.

The suggestion is that she puts up a trellis on top of her wall. This can scarcely be regarded as a revolutionary idea; it may well have occurred to her before; indeed it may already be in position, and she may well be standing in front of it, wondering what to do about it. I will tell her, if she will be so kind as to take out her pencil and write down, at the top of the page, these two words . . .

Climbing Annuals

The climbing annuals are among the most strangely neglected plants in the garden, and they might have been specially created for the elderly. And though no author should ever quote from his own works, I am going to break this rule by recalling a letter which I published in a previous book,[1] because it is so very apposite to this discussion.

I am an old-age pensioner with a mother—eighty-six—who is bedridden and never comes downstairs. We live in a new house with bare walls and I do so long for her to have some flowers to look in through her window, particularly at this time of year [October 15]. All her

[1] *Garden Open Today* (London: Jonathan Cape, 1963).

life, till we came here, she had flowers looking in at her window, she said she liked them best because they seemed so friendly. But we have very little money to spare so if it could be something I could grow from seed so much the better. And it would have to be quick too —at her age. Please, is there anything you can recommend?

The plant I recommended to this nice old person was *Cobaea scandens*, which has a number of pretty pseudonyms, such as Cathedral Bells, Cups and Saucers and Fairy Lanterns. It is like a dark purple Canterbury Bell, and grows at a phenomenal pace, clinging to the wall with its own tendrils. The result of this suggestion could not have been happier, as I was to learn a year later, from another letter:

We did what you said, Mr Nichols, and sowed the seed in the spring, and got a dozen lovely plants. It's just a year since I wrote to you and the flowers *are* looking in to my mother's window and she says they remind her of the Canterbury Bells that used to grow in the garden when she was a girl. And to think that it was all for 1s. 6d.!

Since this homely little episode, I have learned that there is a white variety of the *Cobaea scandens*, which for some mysterious reason had eluded me. Apart from the colour, it has all the amiable qualities of the purple sort. It is of the greatest elegance, producing flowers of white and pale green, which can often be picked as late as mid-November.

Is Mrs P.-S. beginning to cheer up? I hope so, for this is a true story of an old lady of eighty-six—no, eighty-seven— and she has a long way to go before she reaches that sort of age. By the time she does reach it, she will have no need for a trellis at all.

Meanwhile, here are a few more ideas for her to consider . . .

Tropaeolum peregrinum. This is the climbing nasturtium, popularly known as the Canary Creeper. I find it very endearing and 'cottage' and it certainly grows like mad, so that it needs to be visited every two or three days to be kept in order.

Ipomoea rubro-caerula (Morning Glory). These are at last coming into their own in this country, largely, I suspect, because so many people nowadays take their holidays abroad. They see a cascade of blue falling through the railings of a villa on the Costa Brava, and they are so enraptured that they filch a few seeds, looking anxiously over their shoulders in case they should be apprehended by the Spanish police. They take them home and plant them, never expecting them to come up, but they do—and that is the beginning of a love affair. Doubtless Mrs P.-S. will be acquainted with the brilliant blue variety of this flower, but she may not be aware that they also come in magenta, white and wine-red. She may also be unaware that although they need a dry soil they do not need to be drenched in perpetual sunshine, indeed they seem to welcome a little shade. If they are in full sunshine the flowers are inclined to shrivel by the middle of the morning.

Humulus japonicus. Less romantic, but even more effective as a quick trellis-screen, is this Japanese Hop. You can buy seeds of this for a shilling a packet, and if you sow it correctly—with further references to the appendix—it should have climbed to a height of fifteen feet by the end of the summer. Old-fashioned garden writers, such as the immortal

William Robinson, described the Japanese Hop as 'perfect for bowers', and 'admirable for shady nooks and quiet retreats'. The description is, perhaps, questionable, because this hop sometimes attracts large quantities of caterpillars which might mar the perfection of the bowers, should Mrs P.-S. decide to recline in them. But its growth is so vigorous, and its pale green leaves so large and sturdy, that it would need an inordinate number of caterpillars to destroy its effectiveness as a screen.

These climbers that we have been considering are all annuals, swift to come and swift to go. And when they do go, our friend will feel melancholy at their departure. But her sadness will be softened if she has taken the precaution in the meantime to install other, more permanent, residents. The list of these is very long, and I have deliberately excluded climbing roses, not only because they do not form a really satisfactory screen, but because nothing will stop Mrs P.-S. from planting roses anyway. Retired persons with independent incomes, who have nothing else to do, invariably plant roses, and go on planting roses till the cows come home. It must do something for their souls. Ignoring the rose addicts, I will make only two further suggestions:

Clematis and Honeysuckle

Let us show what happens—again taking my own garden as an example—when you put up a trellis, plant clematis beneath it, and a screen of conifers in front. The first thing that happens is that you have 'words' with the person next door. The person in my case was a quite nice old gentleman —he has since departed to another part of the world—who was very angry when he saw my trellis rearing its head above the wall. I told him that he would like it very much indeed when it was covered with clematis. He pointed out that it might be a very long time before this happened, and that meanwhile he did not like it at all; it was bright green and it was covered with nothing. Time, I said, would alter all that. Solicitors, he suggested, might alter it more effectively. It was his wall as much as mine, he said . . . or did he say that it was my wall as much as his? Neither of us was very good at walls or very prone to solicitors. You will probably find that your neighbours are the same. All that you can be quite certain about in the matter of a garden wall is that if it falls down you will be the one who has to pay for it. This is a law of nature.

Anyway, it blew over. Not the wall, but the 'words'. And the clematis did climb like mad, and in two years it was a triumphant blaze of pale pink. The variety we chose was *Clematis montana rubens*, and though it is rash to claim that any plant is 'fool-proof' we should need to be quite exceptionally foolish to fail with this one. Moreover it has the great advantage that it is thickest and most luxuriant *at the top*. As the years go by, and as the conifers gradually shut out the light, the lower branches become bare, which will not matter, because they will no longer be visible. But meanwhile, the upper branches flourish exceedingly, and even in the winter, when the blossoms and the leaves have fallen, there will be such a closely woven mesh of tiny twigs that even though it lets through the light, it will still block out the view. Cross my heart.

The honeysuckles, which we also recommended, will blend very sweetly with the clematis and these too, for the elderly, have a special point of merit, for all the honeysuckles flower in their first year. All the honeysuckles! When I first began to garden I knew only one—the popular *Lonicera*

Periclymenum, whose pale green leaves are among the first tokens of spring in our woodlands. Since then, many other honeysuckles have come into my life. Here are three of them:

Lonicera americana. This is trained over the little front-door porch of the cottage, and is so prim and proper, so completely in period, that it suggests the opening of a chapter from Cranford, with the ladies of the village changing their shoes outside the door, while the linkman held up his lantern among the blossoms.

Lonicera Tellmanniana. The brightest yellow of all, and one of the most vigirous, but with very little scent.

Lonicera Periclymenum serotina. Popularly known as Late Dutch because it flowers at least three weeks after the others. It is also darker in shade and very sweetly scented.

For those who are obliged to economize it is worth while remembering that all the honeysuckles can easily be grown from seed.

And here we will leave Mrs Peebles-Smith, hoping that we have given her enough to think about, in the years that still lie ahead.

'Age'—so I was recently informed by a high-thinking young journalist—'is a state of mind.' That is one way of looking at it. However, age is also a state of double-chins, receding hair-lines, at least one false tooth and—when one visits the tailor—of things going out which used to go in. All this is sad, but it need not too greatly depress us as far as the garden is concerned, particularly if we have followed the advice in the foregoing pages. When we are safely screened from the world we need not bother about holding up our chins or pulling in our tummies, and if we cannot get used to the one false tooth we can take it out and prop it up on the rustic bird table.

But in one sense, age *is* a state of mind . . . a seasonal sense. Even if we knew that this spring was to be our last, that would be no reason for seeing a shadow in the sunshine on the lawn. As a young man, I was so obsessed with the idea that life must go on for ever that when I bought a house with a 999 years' lease I could not settle down at all. Only 999 years? It was ridiculous. It was hardly worth planting the hyacinths. So I sold the house, at a staggering loss, and bought a freehold.

Today, there are only four years to run on my present cottage but that does not greatly worry me. It is a Crown lease and I believe that when one has a Crown lease they let one renew it—whoever 'they' may be—provided that one does not do anything particularly outrageous, like burning public effigies of the Queen. We shall see. In the meantime I shall continue to plant not only the hyancinths but the tulip-trees. They may not flower for me in this world; but—stranger things have happened—they may flower for me in the next.

APPENDIX

Garden Open Today included an appendix in which were listed the names and addresses of the various nurserymen who had supplied the flowers, shrubs and horticultural miscellania described in the book. Judging by the comments of readers, this seems to have been of practical value, particularly as a number of the items mentioned were somewhat hard to come by. So here is another appendix. In order to avoid any charge of favouritism or hidden advertising, I must emphasize that the list is entirely personal. It is merely one man's record of the people who have served him well, and whom he wishes to thank.

If any of the nurserymen I have mentioned are unable to meet the reader's requirements—or indeed, whenever any gardener has difficulty in finding any plant whatsoever—he is recommended to write to the Plant Finder Service which has lately been established by the Horticultural Trades Association. If a plant is rare, or in very limited supply, this excellent organization will tell him where to get it. The address is:

> Plant Finder Service,
> Horticultural Trades Association,
> Cereal House,
> Mark Lane,
> London, EC3.

Doubtless, if I had lived in another part of the country, on another sort of soil, the list would have been quite different. However, by and large, the recommendations in the following pages are independent of local conditions, and may be safely followed by the average reader. This certainly applies to the first item:

Q.R.

These mystic letters stand for 'Quick Results', and the title is more than justified. When the previous book was published, five years ago, I was only just beginning to experiment with this magic formula, and although it seemed to be doing something very exciting, I did not know enough about it to feel justified in singing its praises in public. Today, the situation is different.

The phrase 'magic formula' has a factual basis, and the manner in which I stumbled upon it is not without interest. At about the time that *Garden Open Today* was being put together I was also assembling the facts for a volume of a very different nature which eventually burst upon the world under the title *Powers That Be*. This was a detailed and highly technical study of various aspects of extra-sensory perception, in its latest manifestations, and it was received by the press and the public with what might be described as 'a silence that could be felt'. It was felt by the author, at any rate, for it had taken six years to write; it had involved a great deal of back-breaking research; and it was disheartening that so few people seemed to care tuppence about facts which were, to me, of great importance. However, such are the ups and downs of the literary profession.

The enquiries entailed in the compilation of *Powers That Be* took me far and wide, in time and space . . . to the early experiments of Mesmer and his 'baquet', to the telepathic investigations of Professor Rhine in America's Duke University, to the strange genius of Professor Maby, whose revolutionary treatise 'Physics of the Divining Rod' opened up new worlds which orthodox physicists still seem reluctant to explore, to the even stranger genius of Australia's Evelyn Penrose, who discovers minerals through the medium of a pendulum suspended over a map, and through the incredibly complicated and still largely inexplicable techniques being practised at the de la Warr Laboratories in Oxford. These may be described—very roughly indeed—as a scientific development of Doctor Abrams's 'Black Box', which caused such a furore in medical circles towards the end of the twenties. Needless to say, in trying to reach any sort of logical or authoritative conclusions from such a hotch-potch of baffling material I had set myself an impossible task; if ever there was a case of a fool rushing in where angels feared to tread, this was it. And yet I went on, because there seemed to be a unifying light somewhere, if only I could track it down; and always I had a strange presentiment that I might find it shining in the garden.

It was this presentiment which led me eventually to the experiments of May Bruce, and to her strange, indeed uncanny, garden that lay in a secret corner of the Cotswolds. I had long heard of these experiments, which were a development of the theories of Rudolf Steiner, but it was not until I actually visited her garden that I saw them come to life. She was already a very frail old lady; the garden was neglected and overgrown; but there were things happening in it which could only be described as miraculous. In particular, there was a clump of *Campanula lactiflora*—a modest and amiable flower, normally reaching a height of about three feet—which had leapt to a height of over *nine* feet, and was of such a glowing, resounding blue that you could almost hear the chiming of the bells.

The extraordinary growth of this flower, and of many other flowers and vegetables in the garden, flourishing with a vigour such as I had never seen before, was due to the compost in which it was planted, and—here we come to the point of a story that has already stretched to inordinate lengths—the secret of this compost (which Miss Bruce somewhat vaguely describes as 'radionic') was revealed to her in a dream. One day, so her story goes, she woke up in the morning with a phrase of nine words running through her head: *The Divinity within the flower is sufficient of itself*. This phrase, to her, had only one interpretation—that life comes from life, and that all the vitality needed to strengthen the life of plants comes from other plants. There and then she began to experiment with herbal juices—dandelion, nettle, camomile, yarrow, valerian—adding, apparently at random, infusions of oak bark and even drops of honey, all the while feeling, as she herself confessed, 'not unlike an alchemist weaving spells in a medieval laboratory'.

At last, after a long series of trials and errors, her solution was perfected, and bottled in a row of jars, ready to be applied to a common-or-garden pile of compost, whose principal ingredient was the cuttings from the lawn. One vital question remained. In what *proportion* should the solution be used? She tried one in thirty, one in sixty, one in a hundred. And then, urged by an impulse, one in ten thousand.

Miss Bruce, as I was to learn, was convinced that the 'impulse' which caused her to make this extraordinary and apparently nonsensical decision was dictated by a psychic control.

Within five days the contents of one of the jars had gone ahead and was changing colour rapidly. After ten days she invited a soil expert to come and see the progress of the experiment and place the jars according to their merit. When he made his choice, and examined the labels, this was the result:

> *First:* One in ten thousand.
>
> *Second:* One in a hundred.
>
> *Third:* One in sixty.

This, to me, is one of the most dramatic episodes in the history of gardening. For though we may dismiss the 'dream' and scoff at the 'impulse', and though we may choose to regard the whole episode as a sort of spiritualist-homeopathic fluke, we are still faced with the hard commercial facts of the sequel.

I quote from *Powers That Be*[1]:

The fame of Miss Bruce's activator, and the stories of the magical effect it was having on the compost heaps in her garden, spread far and wide. A great many important people began to wend their way down the shadowy lanes that led to her old rambling home, and she began to find that she was likely to make a great deal of money.

But she did not want a great deal of money. Not for herself, at least. She had the little that satisfied her needs, which were simple enough—to live among things that were green and growing, to make them grow greener and stronger, and at the end of the day to sit in the garden and listen to the song of the birds.

So she gave her secret to a great commercial firm, whose managing director happened to be, as she was, an idealist. Today you can buy it on the market, where it competes with conspicuous success against a vast array of products with the same pretensions. Whether it has quite the same potency in its mass-produced form, I do not know. I have the feeling that there may have been a special personal magic in that old lady's fingers, and that conceivably some of the magic may have been lost in the inevitable hurly-burly of commerce. It remains an exceptionally powerful fertilizer. For I can never forget the sight of those campanulas, those flowers surging up to the sky from their bed of lusty compost,[2]

[1] By kind permission of the publishers, Jonathan Cape Ltd.
[2] A practical exposition of Miss Bruce's methods of compost-making was published by Faber & Faber in 1943: *From Vegetable Waste to Fertile Soil* by May Bruce, 3s. 8d. post free. This is a book that can be given to any jobbing gardener, written as it is in down-to-earth prose, with no psychic frills about it.

singing a song of praise in a shade of electric blue.

In case your local shop does not stock Q.R. it can be obtained direct from the makers . . .

Chase Organics Ltd,
Shepperton,
Middlesex.

A few shillings will buy enough to treat a year's compost in a garden of one acre.

Camellias

Because the first chapter seemed to be getting far too long I omitted any mention of the camellias, which were among the most striking examples of plants which survived the rigours of the winter. None was in the smallest degree affected. And yet, until fairly recently, camellias were regarded as too delicate to be risked outside the protection of a cold greenhouse, and vast expanses of glass were erected to shelter them in stately homes all over the country. The most impressive display I ever saw was at Long Eaton, the home of the late Duke of Westminster, who erected a camellia conservatory which from a distance looked like a miniature Crystal Palace. On week-ends he had a habit of taking his guests for walks after Sunday luncheon, and tearing off great branches for them to carry back to London. This was agony to watch, but one was consoled by the thought that for the next few weeks one's small apartment would gleam with unaccustomed opulence. One cannot have too many camellias, just as one cannot have too much caviar, and Long Eaton was the only house, in my limited experience of such places, where one had too much of both.

However, we should not associate camellias only with

dukes; there is no reason why they should not spring up all over the suburbs, instead of the eternal laurel, provided that we are prepared to spend a little money and to wait a little time. Large specimens are, admittedly, very expensive indeed, but we can still buy well-potted specimens of 15–18 inches for 27s. 6d. These will be probably delivered in the autumn and can be planted out immediately in their permanent position, but if a cold greenhouse is available it is really wiser to keep them in it, just for the first winter.

The varieties I can recommend from personal experience are:

Camellia x Williamsii Donation. Among the most beautiful of the whole family. An exqusite semi-double pink.

C. japonica alba simplex. Single, pure white, and not at all temperamental.

C. japonica elegans. A very old favourite, silvery pink, with a claret-coloured centre.

C. japonica magnoliaeflora. Double flowers shaped like water-lilies, pale pink turning to white.

Hillier's nurseries at Winchester and John Waterer, Sons & Crisp Ltd, The Floral Mile, Twyford, Berks, who list many new American varieties, should be able to supply the requirements of gardeners in the South of England. Those who live in the North might be wiser to deal locally.

Camellias *can* be grown from seed, but frankly I do not recommend the effort, unless you happen to be very young, very lucky, and endowed with infinite patience. I have tried it, plunging boxes in the earth in shady places and covering them with cloches, but nothing seems to happen in the first year, and very little in the second, except that the cloches get broken, or the wood of the boxes rots.

The main enemy of the flower, of course, is late frost, which turns the petals brown. That is why the position in which you plant camellias is of such vital importance. They must never get the morning sun. Remember this when they are still fifteen inches high, and visualize them a few years hence when their heads will be looking over the wall.

Herbs

In Chapter Four the malevolent herbs were given such prominence that we may feel that the balance should be re-dressed by mentioning one or two of the herbs friendly to man. Although I have no longer any space for growing vegetables, I have always managed to find a little corner for a herb garden, if only for the delight of wandering over to it and picking little bits of green things to nibble, such as a spray of parsley or a leaf of mint.

Perhaps the most useful herb in this corner is lovage, which is strangely neglected in the average British kitchen. It is very easy to grow, in sun or shade, and it has a unique taste, suggestive of smoked celery.

Our other herbs are all pretty common-or-garden . . . chives, fennel, sage, that sort of thing. We never go short of tarragon, because it is essential for omelettes. The true *omelette aux fines herbes* contains only three herbs, tarragon, chives and sage. Incidentally, you can make your own tarragon vinegar by soaking the leaves in ordinary white wine vinegar for a fortnight. We also ensure a good supply of dill, which gives a savour of elegant sophistication to the simplest white sauce. And we grow several sorts of mint, not only the ordinary spear-mint for making mint sauce, but also the pineapple mint, for crushing into fruit-cups during the summer months. Perhaps my favourite is the eau-de-cologne mint, which lives up to its title and makes a charming addition to pot-pourri.

244

APPENDIX

Herbs offer a vast field of study; we could plant a whole acre with them and still be cramped for space. However, there is no need to be deterred by that. The smallest patch of herbs is also a little patch of history. Even when we pick a bunch of parsley we are picking a plant that sprang, in Grecian mythology, from the blood of a hero; a plant that crowned the brows of the victors in the Isthmian games; a plant that was later dedicated to St Peter. Please handle it with becoming reverence, next time you lay it on a slab of butter.

In my own experience, the most rewarding herb garden in the British Isles is the creation of Miss Kathleen Hunter, whose address is Barcaldine House, Connel, Argyll, Scotland. Her catalogue is not only a treasury of rare delights but the reflection of a vigorous and most endearing personality.

Regular visitors to the Chelsea Flower Show will no doubt have noticed the herb garden laid out by The Herb Farm Ltd, Seal, Sevenoaks, Kent, who describe their herbs as 'Culinary, Medicinal and Aromatic'.

Heathers

The two firms specializing in heathers, with whom I have had the happiest dealings, are:

Maxwell & Beale,	John F. Letts,
Naked Cross Nursery,	Foxhollow,
Corfe Mullen,	Westwood Road,
Wimborne,	Windlesham,
Dorset.	Surrey.

The name of the late D. F. Maxwell has long been famous in 'the heather world'—if we may presume the existence of such a charming domain. His book *The English Heather Garden*,[1] completed after his death by his constant companion Paul Patrick, is essential reading for all those who wish to explore this world.

John F. Letts is a smaller firm, but no less reputable, and I shall always have a special fondness for it because here I first discovered two of the most beautiful heathers ever grown. The first *Erica cinerea* Golden Drop was introduced by Maxwell & Beale, and Maxwell wrote of it: 'I consider this to be the finest coloured-foliage heath of any species I have yet seen. During summer and autumn the foliage is golden-bronze, and as winter advances the colour changes to red until, by late winter, it is an intense red, brighter than a burning bush.'

All this is true. But when Maxwell wrote in such glowing terms about Golden Drop, had he encountered *Calluna vulgaris* Golden Feather? He does not mention it in his book, although it is even more beautiful. Never was a plant more aptly named. It really is gold—shimmering, eighteen-carat gold, freshly minted. And it really is shaped like a feather. Since Maxwell does not mention it, I assume that it is a newcomer. At any rate it is new to me, and—unless you happen to spend your life in a heather nursery, permanently crouched over beds of experimental cuttings—it will probably be new to you.

Gold in the garden is worth a lot more than gold in the bank, and Golden Feather, I repeat, is sheer gold. And just as money breeds money, so, in the garden, gold magnifies gold. Which is why I have placed my bed of Golden Feather in the vicinity of a golden cypress and interplanted it with

[1] *The English Heather Garden* by D. Fyfe Maxwell and P. S. Patrick (London: Macdonald, 1966).

clumps of Spanish iris Le Mogol, which have golden tongues springing from sepia throats. (At the risk of sounding irrelevant, that description makes me think of chain-smoking millionaires, drifting round the Mediterranean in the company of celebrated *prima donnas*.)

PRACTICAL NOTE

Golden Feather heathers are best increased by layering, but until they have established themselves it is best to leave them alone until the second year.

At the moment of writing they are still rather expensive —ten shillings a plant—but never could money be better spent.

Primula Vialii

I buy my seed from the admirable firm of Thompson & Morgan, which was established in Ipswich well over a century ago. *Primula Vialii* comes at two shillings a packet. It cannot be too often emphasized that the seeds of all primulas are inclined to be tricky; if they are kept too long in store they lose their viability, which is another way of saying—as my first old gardener used to observe—that they don't 'coom oop'. This is not likely to happen in the case of so honourable a firm as Thompson & Morgan. At the same time, if you want to be 100 per cent sure that your primulas don't 'coom oop'. This is not likely to happen in the case of is to pick the seeds from the growing plant. How you are going to do this must be left to your own ingenuity and persistence.

Ginkgo biloba

The situation in the nursery-garden world is not unlike

the situation in the world of the antiquaries: there is not enough stock to go round. You can buy everything but time, and as the years go by, and the antique shops are emptied faster and faster by an increasingly rapacious public, they have to be stocked up again with something or other, and it is usually something or other of an inferior quality at an increased price. This does not apply to the nurserymen, who are inclined to be of a somewhat superior moral fibre to members of other professions in general, and to members of the antique business in particular. But even the nurserymen cannot evade the problem of time, and they are obliged to sell young trees at a price which, only a few years ago, they would have charged for old ones. Camellias are a case in point. A fine tub-grown camellia, seven or eight years old, is hard to come by under twenty guineas.

For those who buy their trees by the yard this will be depressing, but it need not unduly intimidate the more sophisticated. One of the surest signs of the amateur, as he walks round the garden, is that when he sees a tree that appeals to him he invariably asks, 'How tall was it when you put it in?' The question now irritates me so much that I usually answer by bending down, holding my hand just above the soil, and replying, 'Three inches.'

Which brings us to the *Ginkgo biloba*. You may not find this in your catalogues, because you may not know how to look it up. Nurserymen's catalogues are essential reading for all gardeners, but in order to get the best out of them they must be supplemented by standard works of reference. The other day an old lady sent me an indignant letter because I had suggested that people might buy their ginkgos from Messrs Jackman & Son, whose nurseries are at Woking in Surrey. 'I *have* their catalogue,' she wrote, 'and they do not even *list* this tree. I really do think that you should *check* your facts before rushing into *print*.' To which I replied that the criticism applied rather more forcibly to herself. She had looked it up under 'Trees and Shrubs' whereas she should have turned to the section devoted to 'Conifers'. If she had been a nice sensible person, instead of such a crotchety old thing, she would have invested in the immortal work of Mr W. J. Bean, whose *Trees and Shrubs Hardy in the British Isles* is still, after many years, a golden treasury of information for every gardener.

However, the old lady had perhaps some excuse for her ignorance. As we observed in our visit to Kew, the ginkgo is a mystery tree, and there is nothing in its appearance which would suggest to the average observer that it is a member of the conifer family. Some fifty years ago, Bean wrote that it is best raised from seed, and if there are still any gardeners around who took his advice, their trees today would be sixty feet high. (Seeds can be obtained from Thompson & Morgan's, Ipswich, at 1s. 6d. a packet.) The price of Jackman's standards is 17s. 6d. for specimens of 2 to 3 feet. I still think that the smaller trees are the best buy.

Echiums and other chalk flowers

In our visit to Sir Frederick Stern's garden we singled out *Echium scilloniensis* as a 'plant for the exhibitionist', but the less spectacular varieties will probably make a more practical appeal to those experimenting for the first time with these charming annuals. Although the dwarf hybrids come in various colours, the basic natural shade of the echium is blue, and for me the *Echium plantagineum* Blue Bedder, at a shilling a packet, is by far the most rewarding.

As for the 'other chalk flowers', what do we mean by a

'chalk flower'? For that matter, what do we mean by 'chalk'? In other words, what precise degree of acidity or alkalinity is implied, and which flowers will flourish in which degrees of one or the other? It would seem that the most obvious way of answering this question is to take a sample of soil, to have it analysed, and to plan one's planting in accordance with the results of the analysis. This sounds nicely clear-cut and 'scientific', but the problem is not quite so simply resolved. Even in a small garden such as mine the quality of the soil has many variations; a sample taken from one corner may differ sharply from a sample taken from another. This is especially noticeable in old gardens, where the ghostly remains of ancient cemented paths still haunt the beds which the new owners have dug for themselves, or where the limy foundations of long-forgotten out-buildings still linger on, to poison the roots of an unsuspecting rhododendron. Against such a combination of history and chemistry and sheer bad luck, the long-suffering horticulturist is impotent.

My own solution to these problems, as to many others, is to go for a walk. There are very few of life's dilemmas—always, of course, excepting the demands of the Inland Revenue Authorities—which cannot be resolved by a nice long walk.

Let us therefore suppose that you are cottage-hunting, that you have decided roughly whereabouts you want to live, and have written to the local house-agents, asking them to send particulars of suitable properties. (You will, of course, realize that writing to house-agents initiates a correspondence that lasts for life. House-agents never give in. Long after they have been informed that one is comfortably settled, their brochures continue to arrive, bearing details of the same 'desirable residences' which have been inspected and rejected years ago. Although I have been at my present address for ten years I still receive impassioned pleas to purchase cottages which are endowed with 'a wealth of old oak'. I wish they would realize that I do not want a cottage, least of all one which has a wealth of old oak. There must be some way of imparting this information to the world in general, and to house-agents in particular. Perhaps one should put it in *Who's Who*.) Your next move takes place on a Sunday afternoon when, suitably clad for walking, you repair to the area of your choice.

In a moment we will be setting out, but first I want you to do yourself a favour and buy a book: *A Concise British Flora in Colour* by W. Keble Martin.[1] Since it has sold over 100,000 copies you may already possess a copy; even so, you may not have read it as it was intended to be read, in the open air. In the *Concise British Flora* we have one of the most romantic episodes in publishing history. It was published when the author was well into his eighties, and is the result of a lifetime of research under conditions of great difficulty, during days snatched from his regular duties as a parish priest. Often after a busy Sunday, in which he had conducted Holy Communion, preached a sermon at morning service and taken Evensong single-handed, he would catch a late train to some new area of exploration, travelling at times as far afield as Scotland. All through the years he was busy with his pencil and paintbox, re-creating the wild flowers of our country with exquisite draughtsmanship and impeccable accuracy. The results, glowing in natural colour—nearly 1400 of them—are to be found in this volume, which is a floral treasury if ever there was one.

[1] *A Concise British Flora in Colour* by W. Keble Martin, with a Foreword by H.R.H. the Duke of Edinburgh (London: George Rainbird, 1965).

We can now set out on our walk, clutching the *Concise British Flora* under our arm. The purpose of this promenade is to acquaint ourselves not only with the lie of the land, but the quality, the composition, one might almost say the *atmosphere* of the land. Just as every city has its atmosphere, which is quite independent of its size, its prosperity, or its architecture, so—I like to think—has every stretch of virgin land, every field and hill and valley. However, if we were to develop this theory we should find ourselves in psychic territory, which is not our present destination. All that we need to know is the degree of alkalinity or acidity of the land on which we propose to live, and this we can discover far more satisfactorily by studying the wild flowers around us than by submitting the soil to scientific analysis.

Plants of Alkaline Soils

Clematis Vitalba. This is the Old Man's Beard of one's childhood, whose feathery fruits drift through the autumn hedgerows like plumes of smoke from a bonfire of burning leaves. Whenever you see these spectral symbols, it is a fairly safe bet that your feet are treading on chalky soil.

This clematis is the first illustration on Plate 1 of the *Concise British Flora*, so you should have no difficulty in finding it and—I hope—marvelling at the enchanting way in which it springs to life on the printed page.

Atropa belladonna. The Deadly Nightshade. When I was a child, and first heard this lurid title from the lips of my old governess, I felt the same sort of *frisson* that Shelley must have felt on hearing the spine-chilling passage from 'The Ancient Mariner' . . .

Like one, that on a lonesome road

Doth walk in fear and dread,
And having once turned round walks on
And turns no more his head;
Because he knows, a frightful fiend
Doth close behind him tread.

Shelley—predictably—swooned. I did not. But the phrase 'Deadly Nightshade' has never lost its power to shock; it still glimmers at the back of my mind with an evil glow: like a figure on a darkening stage, in robes of sickly purple, bearing berried fruits of poisoned blood.

You will find it on Plate 61. Although it is beautifully drawn, it will not—we hope—make you swoon. But it *will* tell you, once again, that you are treading on chalky soil. And it will also tell you—particularly if you should happen to be accompanied by a child who might be attracted by the glitter of the berries—that you are in dangerous territory.

Scabiosa Columbaria. This is the pretty, pale mauve flower which might be described as a miniature edition of the annual garden scabious, which has now been developed in many pleasing shades. Plate 43 of the *Concise British Flora.*

Origanum vulgare. The popular name for this is marjoram, and there is a very life-like picture of it on Plate 67 of our book. It grows about nine inches tall, with clusters of pale rose flowers, and it is one of the surest indications that there is chalk nearby.

Thymus Serpyllum. This is the common wild thyme. When Shakespeare wrote, 'I know a bank whereon the wild thyme blows,' he was not only writing a line of poetry; he was giving a clear indication that he lived in a chalky district. The next three lines do nothing to contradict this impression:

Where oxlips and the nodding violet grows
Quite over-canopied with luscious woodbine,
With sweet musk-roses and with eglantine. . . .

All these are 'alkaline' flowers, although they will also flourish in acid conditions. Shakespearean scholars have doubtless scrutinized the flora of the plays, but I know of nobody who has discussed them in a botanical connection. This might provide a modern producer with some interesting opportunities for 'realistic expressionism'. For example, when Bottom roused himself from his dream, it would be quite legitimate to provide him with a white patch on his behind.

Now for some trees. We do not need to study the *Concise British Flora* to read the message of the trees; we do not even have to get out of the car; they proclaim the nature of their environment for all to see. Here are four of the safest guides:
Fagus sylvatica. The Common Beech. The great W. J. Bean had a special fondness for this tree, and made journeys all over the British Isles to study individual examples. All the finest specimens were growing on chalk. And though the beech also flourishes on an acid soil it is significant that the most impressive beech forest in our country is Savernake Forest, within sight of the solid chalk downs of Wiltshire.
Euonymus europaeus. The Spindle Tree.
Sorbus Aria. The Whitebeam.
Thelycrania sanguinea. The Dogwood.

All of them predominantly 'alkaline' trees, though the spindle is perhaps more fittingly described as a shrub. If these provide the main arboreal features of the landscape, the overwhelming odds are that you are on chalk. And if you ever had an idea of growing a rhododendron, forget it.

The reader may begin to suspect that I have an obsession about the nature of the soil. 'Know thy soil' is as vital an injunction to the gardener as 'Know thyself' to the philosopher, and it is only with a great effort that I refrain from developing the theme that between the soil and the self there is a very real psychic link. Before the effort becomes too painful I will hastily compile another brief list.

Plants of Acid Soil

Calluna vulgaris and *Erica sp.* The mystic 'sp' is really a bit of camp. It stands for 'species' and is only put in to give an air of lofty authority. The average non-botanical person will probably be content to bracket the calluna and the various ericas under the single title of 'heather', though the calluna is in fact the common ling. If you want to be high-hat about it you can turn up the *Concise British Flora*, and read the learned author's description: '*Erica Tetralix*. Cross-leaved heath. Leaves 4 in whorl; margins revolute to mid-rib; anthers awned. Common on boggy heaths.'

Every vestige of lofty authority would be stripped from me if I were to confess that the phrase 'margins revolute to mid-rib' immediately conjured up the vision of a strip-tease dancer, but these little irrelevancies sometimes help to jog the memory. If I were ever to find myself stranded with a *real* botanist, in the centre of a blasted heath, I should certainly bring it lightly into the conversation. I might even follow it up with 'common on boggy heaths'. Whether the erica are on, or off, boggy heaths, the adjective 'common' seems inapposite.

Rumex Acetosella. Known to country people as Sheep's Sorrel and a sure indication of acidity. However, this is a modest and retiring little plant, which you may be

inclined to overlook. An easier clue is afforded by . . .
Lychnis Flos-cuculi. The Ragged Robin, whose pale rose petals
bring a glimmer of gaiety, even on the darkest days, to the
hedgerows that skirt the lanes of Devonshire and Cornwall.
Campanula rotundifolia. The Harebell. In Scotland this is called
the bluebell, although it bears no resemblance to the blue-
bells of the rest of Britain which, of course, are a form of wild
hyacinth. It is worth studying this carefully in our book,
because there are other campanulas—tolerant of chalk—
which might perhaps be confused with it.
Sarothamnus scoparius. The common broom. The plate on
which the brooms are illustrated in the *Concise British Flora*
is one of the prettiest in the whole volume, glowing with
yellow blossom, so vividly drawn that the page seems to
carry a faint scent of honey. It is also one of the most rewarding, because these members of the pea family are easily confused, and some—like the gorses—are no proof of acidity.

Among plants indicating acidity are various rushes and
grasses, but since these are usually to be found on heaths—
which will already have announced their acid character—
it seems unnecessary to list them.

Trees

Once again the trees tell the story most swiftly and dramatically. As soon as you have acquired what might be
described as the 'taste' of acidity on your palate, the trees
will give the necessary reassurance as soon as you have
escaped from the clutches of chalk. Not only the silver
birches, which are perhaps the safest guide, and the sweet
chestnuts, but the oaks, for though oaks can cope with a
certain amount of alkalinity, it is only in acid conditions
that they grow to their full and royal stature. The same

256

applies to most of the conifers; as soon as their roots reach chalk they lose their lustre, their growth is stunted and often —particularly in the case of Scotch firs—they die or fall victims to the gales. Whereas, on an acid foundation, they flourish and rejoice.

Postscript

Of all the sections of this book, the foregoing passages are the most easily open to contradiction. There can be no hard-and-fast rules to tell us the precise nature of the soil with 100 per cent accuracy, for the very simple reason that few stretches of land—particularly in an ancient country where every county has been ploughed by the furrows of history—are in a virgin condition. Even on an open moorland there may be limy traces, marking the tracks of long-forgotten roads. Apart from that, plants, like people, are often unpredictable. Just as the student of biology finds himself at times confronted by human beings who appear to flourish on diets which, by rights, should kill them, so the student of botany is confronted by plants which flourish in conditions which seem to break all the accepted rules. There is always an 'X Force' in Nature, and I doubt whether either the biologists or the botanists will ever be able to assess it in its true potential.

The Poison Problem

One's attitude to the whole vexed question of the use of poisons in the garden is determined to no small extent by one's own personality. Some are born poisoners, some achieve poison, and some—the majority of us—have poison thrust upon them. Perhaps it may not be too fanciful to see a connection between the poisoners and the capital punishers; both belong to the class of person who, when confronted by a nuisance, are inclined to say 'off with its head', and leave it at that.

It would be unfair to suggest that the indiscriminate poisoners are morally inferior to those who eschew poison, or only use it with the greatest reluctance. We are not *born* with a sense of the exquisite balance of Nature's fabric; we do not feel, as children, that nothing was ever created without good reason; nor are we endowed with an instinctive sense of the dangers inherent in wholesale destruction. Such convictions come slowly and painfully, as a result of study and research, and the literature on this very specialized subject is as yet sparse and uncollated. The warning voices are few and far between. For example, our natural reaction to the insect world is one of hostility; insects are 'creepy-crawlies' to be squashed or swatted; 'the only good bug is a dead bug'. And yet . . .

Insects are vital to the very existence of higher life. Without them, the endless cycles of life, death, decay and birth, could not possibly function. Even in temperate climates it is doubtful whether microbes and bacteria, unaided by insects, could cope with the enormous mass of dead plant and animal materials. But the larvae of many wood-inhabiting beetles, ants, termites and springtails shred the leaves, chew up the twigs, tear apart the trunks of fallen trees, and devour dead animal tissue, which is then further broken down by soil organisms and returned to the soil to serve as nutrients. In turn, the insects die and become food for predators. In the tropics, this breakdown process is even more important. If it were not for the work of insects, the forests would soon become choked by accumulated dead timber, vegetation and animal life.

The above extract is taken from a book which is compulsive reading for anybody who has ever sprayed a bed of roses —*Gardening Without Poisons* by Beatrice Trum Hunter.[1] It backs up Rachel Carson's *Silent Spring* with a wealth of statistical information, and although it was originally written for American readers its lessons apply with equal cogency to the gardeners of England or indeed of any country in the world.

My own feeling, as far as the gardening fraternity is concerned, is that we should all be a great deal better off if the scientists did a brisk about-turn, lowered their telescopes, ceased to scan the skies of the future, and reopened the pages of the past. After all, there is no aroma of D.D.T. in the pages of Jane Austen but her gardens are no less fragrant for the lack of it. The flower-pieces which delight us in the masterpieces of the great Dutch painters of the seventeenth century are often buzzing with insects—caterpillars, beetles, moths, ladybirds and dragon-flies—and sometimes I fancy that the artists inserted them not only for their beauty but in order to remind us that they are a vital element in the immensely intricate pattern woven by the supreme artist, Nature herself. As Scott observed in *Marmion*, 'The rose is sweetest washed in morning dew.'

This line of poetry might serve to bring us down to earth. In Chapter Eight I mentioned how a row of lavender bushes, infected by frog-hoppers, had been cleansed by hosing with pure water. I was therefore interested to read in Mrs Hunter's book that she regards water as the simplest and least toxic

[1] *Gardening Without Poisons. A Constructive Answer to the Pesticide Problem* by Beatrice Trum Hunter (London: Hamish Hamilton, 1965). By kind permission of the publishers.

spray of all, for washing off young cabbage-worms, dis-lodging mealy bugs, and even eliminating red spider mites by persistent syringing of the under-leaves. Water is of special value in the greenhouse; small plants infected with aphids are effectively and permanently cleansed by being briefly plunged in water at $125°$ F.

And speaking of greenhouses may we gently remind the reader that it is not really vital to turn these pleasant retreats, every so often, into miniature replicas of the gas-chambers of Belsen and Dachau. We do not need to emulate Hitler in order to fumigate a greenhouse. The smoke of oak-leaves—which are not poisonous, do not kill soil bacteria, and leave no harmful residue—does the job just as well. A simple home fumigator can be made in a bucket lined with newspapers, equipped with a little metal grating on which is spread a layer of straw. When the leaves are piled into the straw they should be sprinkled with water to prevent them burning too quickly.

It is a pity that the aforesaid Dutch masters of the seven-teenth century never painted any pictures of their tool-sheds, showing how contemporary gardeners went about their business. We might have learned a great deal from a study of their shelves. There would have been bags of salt for weed-control, jars of skimmed milk for spraying against mosaic virus, and many mysterious bottles which, if we could read the labels, would throw a new—or rather a very old—light on the mysterious balances and counterbalances of Nature's therapies. Nasturtium juice for washing into the internodes of twigs, eucalyptus oil for painting on infested trees, crushed tomato leaves soaked in water for use on the peach-trees, baskets of leaves from the Virginia creeper to carry out to the orchard for rubbing on the trunks of the apples, tincture of rhubarb as a preventative against club-root and black spot, even jars of the water in which their wives had boiled the potatoes. (Apparently, the potato flour in the water had an adhesive function and turned the leaves of the affected plant into a sort of benevolent fly-paper.) Precisely how such nostrums were employed, in what proportions, and with what degree of effectiveness, we may never know, but one would have thought, in all humility, that by turning back to a study of these ancient pages of horticultural history the modern chemist might refresh his memory and—just possibly—discover something that he had overlooked, or rediscover something he had forgotten.

And if these old painters had wandered out from their tool-sheds to the gardens, taking their sketchbooks with them, it would not have been only the flowers that caught their fancy; the insects, the birds, the frogs—even the worms —would have been transferred to their pages. A bee lighting on a Canterbury Bell, performing the vital service of pollination. A ladybird nestling in the heart of a chrysanthemum, elegantly nibbling away at the aphids. A martial trail of ants, setting out to protect their nests from a foray of fruit-flies. A toad by the edge of the lily-pond, casting a baleful eye at the gardener's enemies that flock in from all the corners of the earth and the heavens. A toad, let it never be forgotten, can eat up to 10,000 insects in the space of twelve weeks. It also consumes:

> Grubs
> Rose chafers
> Squash bugs
> Sow bugs
> Tent caterpillars
> Armyworms

Potato beetles
Flies
Mosquitoes

I seem—inadvertently—to have compiled a comprehensive list of the young persons who charm the modern generation through the medium of pop music. It would be pleasant to think that they might be as easily eliminated as their prototypes in the insect world.

Scented Lawns

As this is a somewhat specialized branch of horticulture, it is important that you should deal with a firm who will give you individual attention. I can recommend

Treneague Chamomile Farm,
Wadebridge,
Cornwall.

Since we have evoked the perfume of the scented lawns, this might be an occasion to suggest that, for the elderly, the whole subject of fragrance in the garden is one to which more attention might be given. The sense of smell is one of the last to desert us and it can give delight and consolation to the end of our lives. Moreover it involves no physical effort. One has yet to hear of anybody dying of exhaustion of the nostrils.

New scents are impossible to imagine in the mind or to transfer to the printed page, but sometimes one does encounter a scent which one has never savoured before. New to me until a couple of years ago, and maybe still undiscovered by many gardeners, was the unique aroma of the *Eucalyptus citriodora*. An Australian reader sent me a packet of seed, with no cultural directions and, indeed, no sort of indication of what it was, beyond observing that it would give me 'a pleasant surprise'. It did. We sowed it in October in the cold greenhouse, and by the following June we had half a dozen nice little plants whose leaves exuded a bitter-sweet fragrance which is almost hypnotically alluring. It bears scarcely any trace of the familiar essence which we sprinkle on our handkerchiefs when we have a cold—though this flavour, for me, is not unpleasing. As its name implies, the leaves are strongly impregnated with lemon, but there are two points to notice. Firstly, it is the *rind* of the lemon that is predominant, rather than the flower or the juice. Secondly, the lemons quite obviously have been gathered in the Elysian fields, for they carry with them a gentle breath of honey, and the young leaves are faintly silvered, as though they had gathered to them the rays of the rising moon.

The elderly should certainly invest in a packet of these seeds, by sending half-a-crown plus postage to Messrs Thompson & Morgan, Ipswich. While they are about it they might care to order some of the other eucalyptus, of which no less than fourteen are listed in the catalogue. All the eucalyptus grow so swiftly that they might have been specially created for those advanced in years. However, we must be prepared for disaster if the winter is exceptionally severe. The hardiest is *Eucalyptus Gunnii*—the Blue Cider gum. Although my own tree was killed by frost, several fine specimens flourish in other people's gardens only a few miles away, to my great disgust.

One could write a book—indeed one could write several books—on scent in the garden, but fortunately there is no need to do so. The task has already been accomplished with the greatest elegance and erudition by Eleanour Sinclair

Rohde, whose pages are as fragrant as the plants she cele-brates.[1] If the elderly will read it they will learn far more than I could ever teach them and they will, I hope, receive with gratitude the message of the dedication, quoted from the sixteenth-century *Gardners Labyrinth*. This was addressed to the Lord High Treasurer of England, William Cecil, Lord Burghley. It reads:

> I wish unto you by dayly Prayer and fruition of the Heavenly Paradise craving of the Omnipotent and provident God, the guider of that gorgeous Garden that hee would vouchsafe to graunte unto you the sweete savour of his chiefe fragrante floures, that is his comfort to cleave faste unto you, his mercy to keepe you and his grace to guyde you nowe and evermore.

And with these comforting words we will bid the reader —until the next time—a fond farewell.

Hardy Fuchsias can be obtained from:

> L. R. Russell Ltd,
> Richmond Nurseries,
> Windlesham,
> Surrey.

This firm, renowned for fuchsias, list a dozen-and-a-half hardy varieties. Prices from 9s. 6d. to 11s. 6d.

Water-lilies and Waterside Plants

> Perry's Hardy Plant Farm,
> Theobald's Park Road,
> Enfield, Middlesex.

---

[1] *The Scented Garden* by Eleanour Sinclair Rohde (London: the Medici Society, 1931).

Cupressocyparis Leylandii (the Leyland cypress)

> Pennell & Sons Ltd,
> 312 High Street,
> Lincoln.

Specialist growers of the screening conifer.

Silver-foliage Plants

All the silver plants mentioned in Chapter Six are listed by:

> Mrs Desmond Underwood,
> Ramparts Nurseries,
> Braiswick,
> Colchester,
> Essex.

Bulbs

> P. de Jager & Sons (London) Ltd,
> The Nurseries,
> Marden,
> Kent.

Rare and Unusual Perennial Plants

> Bressingham Gardens,
> Diss,
> Norfolk.

Horticultural Sundries

> E. J. Woodman & Sons (Pinner) Ltd,
> 19/25 High Street,
> Pinner,
> Middlesex.

This firm can be of great assistance to those gardeners who are unable to obtain a particular aid to the garden in their local horticultural shop.

Finally, for all seeds of uncommon plants that may not be listed in the average catalogue, the reader is recommended to

Messrs Thompson & Morgan,
Ipswich.

INDEX

The plant names in this index were corrected and updated by Roy C. Dicks. Where necessary, new scientific names have been provided in brackets following the scientific name used in the book.

INDEX